DR. CHERRY WANTS EVERY EXPECTANT
PARENT TO KNOW . . .

As a noted obstetrician, gynecologist, and research pioneer in fetology, Dr. Cherry has personally delivered more than 2,000 babies.

Drawing on his years of experience in a fast-changing field, he now shares reassuring routine information and vital new developments with every concerned parent in a guide that is unique in its clarity, honesty, and scope. In one volume he includes everything the expectant mother needs to know to actively participate in the pregnancy, delivery, and care of her newborn infant.

Adopting the same, gentle, confident, and understanding tone he uses with his own patients, he reassures every pregnant woman that childbirth can be one of the most rewarding and exciting experiences of her lifetime.

UNDERSTANDING PREGNANCY AND CHILDBIRTH

Revised and Updated Edition
by Sheldon H. Cherry, M.D.

BANTAM BOOKS
TORONTO • NEW YORK • LONDON • SYDNEY • AUCKLAND

*This low-priced Bantam Book
has been completely reset in a type face
designed for easy reading, and was printed
from new plates. It contains the complete
text of the original hard-cover edition.*
NOT ONE WORD HAS BEEN OMITTED.

UNDERSTANDING PREGNANCY AND CHILDBIRTH
(REVISED EDITION)

*A Bantam Book / published by arrangement with
The Bobbs-Merrill Co., Inc.*

PRINTING HISTORY

Bobbs-Merrill edition published June 1973
2nd printing . . . . September 1973   3rd printing . . . . . November 1974
Book-of-the-Month Club edition published November 1973
Excerpts appeared in AMERICAN BABY *and* EXPECTING *magazines.*
Bobbs-Merrill revised edition published May 1983

Bantam Edition / December 1975

2nd printing . . . . December 1975	7th printing . . . . May 1978
3rd printing . . . . May 1976	8th printing . . . . April 1979
4th printing . . . . May 1977	9th printing . . . . November 1979
5th printing . . . . August 1977	10th printing . . . . June 1980
6th printing . . . . March 1978	11th printing . . . . June 1981

Bantam revised edition / March 1984
2nd printing . . . . August 1984

Photos courtesy Photofile

ISBN 0-553-23934-1

Published simultaneously in the United States and Canada

---

*Bantam Books are published by Bantam Books, Inc. Its trade-
mark, consisting of the words "Bantam Books" and the por-
trayal of a rooster, is Registered in U.S. Patent and Trademark
Office and in other countries. Marca Registrada. Bantam
Books, Inc., 666 Fifth Avenue, New York, New York 10103.*

PRINTED IN THE UNITED STATES OF AMERICA

O   11 10 9 8 7 6 5 4 3 2

To my family; to my associates, Drs. Herbert Jaffin and Richard Moss; and to my patients.

CONTENTS

FOREWORD

In simpler times, an aura of security and even sanctity surrounded the physician and instilled in his patients great confidence in his authority, optimism about his treatment, and a bond of mutual respect born of having lived through moments of stress together. This era encouraged the physician to be authoritative and even paternalistic in his relations with his patients, for all too often he saw this demeanor as a critical means of psycho-emotional support when the treatment offered had pragmatic evidence of value only, without substantial scientific support.

In the sophisticated urban and suburban society that is now the environment in which most of our population lives and works, this security about health matters is needed more than ever, but it can no longer be derived solely from the physician's image as a healer. Even the obstetrician who was more frequently the object of devotion and love of his patients because he shared with them and supported them in the highest expression of their femininity, the dramatic, romantic moment of childbirth, has found himself cast more often now in the role of teacher than that of medicine man. And this is appropriate in an era when the explosion in biological knowledge has been translated into new understanding of intrauterine fetal life, complex clinical techniques, and electronic instruments that have vastly improved the comfort and safety of pregnancy and childbirth.

With this new more scientific approach to the health of mother and infant has come a concomitant rise in the expectation that the obstetrician and his associated health workers will inform and translate, simplify, and explain pregnancy and childbirth and other reproductive phenomena in a manner suitable to a more educated generation that derives its security from knowledge rather than mystique. With every issue of the public press suggesting new medical advances, the patient demands that her physician and most especially her obstetrician, concerned now with two patients, act not only as confidant but also as guide through the maze of genuine and spurious discoveries so that wise choices can be made with his help between the scientific and the cultist.

Dr. Cherry's updated guide to *Understanding Pregnancy and Childbirth* is a superb presentation of modern obstetrical knowledge in a style that is a model of comprehension and clarity. He chooses to refrain from adhering to a single school of obstetrical management with the thought that childbirth is best served by an informed partnership between the patient and her obstetrician. This movement to ask people to take some responsibility for their own health can only result in better care for the public and better education for the physician. Information will replace ignorance, skill will replace magic, and the bond of commitment between the patient and her physician will be strengthened. This volume will surely attain the wide readership that its substance deserves and will make a real contribution to the well-being of those readers who wish a clear understanding of the modern obstetrical era.

S.B. Gusberg, M.D., D. Sci.
Distinguished Service Professor
Department of Obstetrics
   and Gynecology
The Mount Sinai School of Medicine
New York, New York

ACKNOWLEDGMENTS

In the preparation of this manuscript, I was assisted by Nancy Hicks, a fine writer and recent mother. I also thank Kathleen Hall for writing the chapter on Lamaze technique. And thanks to the Maternity Center Association, New York City, for the use of their excellent illustrations.

Additional thanks to Ann Cristiano for reediting the Lamaze chapter and to Carol Shiroky for her help on the manuscript.

INTRODUCTION

Childbirth, that most natural yet most awesome experience of mankind, has in the past been cloaked in superstition and cultural mystique. These qualities have evolved over the years to fill the vacuum created by a great deal of scientific ignorance about human reproduction. They have added a supernatural and almost fatalistic aura to the regeneration of the human species, a process which is so much more than a biological occurrence.

Expectant parents of past generations have accepted the folk tales of childbirth passed on from generation to generation, modifying them slightly as new facts about human reproduction have become known. They have accepted the perfunctory explanations given their questions by doctors who doubted their patients' ability to understand.

Over the recent past, however, obstetrical care has been changing. The amount of new medical information about childbirth has revolutionized obstetrical practice. While doctors still do not know all the answers to such questions as how two basic cells—one from each parent—combine and form skin, blood, hair, muscles, and so many different human systems, they have learned how to tell the sex of the unborn child, how to detect certain developmental problems in pregnancy, and in some cases how to treat these problems. Young educated adults, who are learning about some of these medical developments in their college science courses, are beginning to demand of their doctors more information about the basic biological aspects of pregnancy.

This book is designed to accommodate these two forces which have come together at this point in time—a great deal of new knowledge and an increasing demand for information.

It includes material never before published in a handbook for parents in addition to all the routine and important information concerning pregnancy such as diagnosis, hygiene, diet, and physical annoyances.

This book will give you specific information about how the fetus develops. The labor and delivery chapter describes much more than signs of labor. It discusses the whole process of labor as an adaptation between mother and baby. It describes the stages of labor, which many women have never heard of before. It discusses in detail the popular Lamaze method of natural childbirth.

There is a chapter on conditions of pregnancy which attempts to explain to the mother-to-be such occurrences as miscarriage and tubal pregnancies so that women can intelligently understand the basic process, its alterations and the risks involved in the common "danger signs of pregnancy." It explains amniocentesis, or analysis of amniotic fluid for abnormalities in pregnant women over 35, since birth defects increase as women approach the end of their childbearing years.

I have included a chapter on chemical and environmental effects on pregnancy which explains, in part, the effect on the fetus of drugs taken during gestation.

There is also a complete review of contraceptive practice—a subject which may not be of interest to you now but will be after the birth of the baby—as well as a discussion of abortion and the changing laws in this country today.

All this information is presented for one purpose: to make childbirth a less mysterious and frightening occurrence, through education. The book holds to no particular dogma. All the current trends in childbirth are discussed, such as breast-feeding and natural birth, complete with appended instructions. But all information is always in context of all options available to the mother and should be used in conjunction with your physician.

Many women shy away from the explicit approach I have tried to use in this complete handbook to modern pregnancy. They do so on the misconception that knowledge detracts from the intuitive beauty of childbirth. This need not be the case. My patients tell me over and over again how much easier and more enjoyable birth is when they know what to expect. Just the difference between thinking of labor as one continuous pain and knowing that a single contraction cannot last longer than 90 seconds means the difference between approaching labor as an unbearable, frightening experience and as a manageable, exciting one. Such knowledge makes the mother a participant in, rather than a victim of, reproduction.

PREFACE TO REVISED EDITION

During the past ten years since the first edition was written, major changes have occurred in obstetrics, changes both in care of the pregnant mother-to-be and of the second patient, the fetus *in utero*. Increasingly, we are more and more concerned about the quality of life for both the mother and the newborn. No longer are obstetricians concerned with just delivering a baby to a healthy mother. We are now concerned that each child be born *well* and what the quality of 70 years or more of life will be for that newborn. We have entered an era in which the fetus is now rightfully considered and treated as our second patient. Fetal diagnosis and therapy have emerged as tools in the hands of obstetricians. Each year, the number of tools the obstetrician can employ increases. The status of fetal health and the well-being and growth of the fetus can be monitored accurately. This is an exciting time for obstetrics because more and more we serve the fetus as physician.

There are many revisions and additions to this second edition. Some of these changes include:

New Concepts on Exercise and Maternal Nutrition.
New Techniques for Early Pregnancy Diagnosis.
Fetal Monitoring—Antepartum and Intrapartum.
Ultrasound Diagnosis.
Management of Complicated Pregnancies.
Amniocentesis Studies.
Genetic Diagnostic Techniques and Prenatal Diagnosis.
Management of Premature Labor and Herpes Infections.
Use of Cesarean Section.
Concepts in Repeat Cesarean Sections.

Advances in Infertility Problems.
Use of Alternative Birthing Methods.
Environmental Hazards.

So join me on this exciting adventure of pregnancy and childbirth. As it unfolds, its knowledge will enable you to participate, understand, and enjoy the unique experience of childbirth.

1
THE PREGNANCY

FERTILIZATION (CONCEPTION)

The moment that male reproductive cell, the sperm, penetrates its female counterpart, the ovum, fetal growth begins. This unheralded union is known as "fertilization" or "conception," and it occurs after sexual intercourse has been engaged in near the time of ovulation.

The Egg

Each month, the female ovary releases into the reproductive tract one egg (ovum) to be fertilized. This release is known as "ovulation." Ovulation takes place about 14 days before the end of the menstrual cycle. A menstrual cycle begins with the first day of the menses and ends with the first day of the next menses. In a 28-day cycle, ovulation would be about day 14, or day 16 in a 30-day cycle.

Once released, the ovum travels by muscular and fluid forces into the Fallopian tubes, the most common site of fertilization, then passes into the uterus. If intercourse is correctly timed and the egg is fertilized, it implants itself into the soft, bloody uterine wall, which has been thickening during the month to receive and nourish the ovum. If the egg is not fertilized, the egg and the uterine lining leave the body. Their exit is called "menstruation." Then the whole cycle begins again the next month.

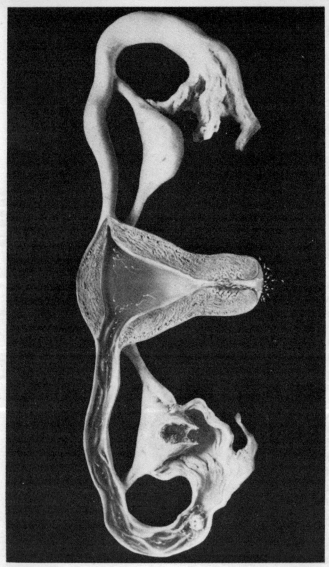

Fertilization: Sperm deposited at cervix swim into the uterus to meet the ovum in the Fallopian tube. *Courtesy Maternity Center Association, New York City.*

Sperm

Millions of sperm cells are thrust into the female reproductive system with each ejaculation by the male during intercourse. If sperm are deposited during the so-called nonfertile period in a woman's menstrual cycle, they swim about ineffectively. But if they are deposited during the fertile period immediately following ovulation, they move from the vagina into the uterus toward the egg, lashing their tails in an effort to meet the ovum in the Fallopian tubes. In their journey, the sperm are protected from the acidity of vaginal secretions by buffers in the ejaculate until they enter the alkaline uterus. Sperm are very fragile, which is why they are manufactured outside the warmth of the body cavity, in the testicle. They can live about two days within a female. Intercourse must occur within 48 hours of ovulation for conception to occur.

Implantation

Five to eight days after conception, the fertilized egg makes a home for itself in the endometrium, the uterine wall. This settling in is called "implantation" and may be accompanied by a small amount of painless vaginal bleeding which lasts a few days. It is in the endometrium that the fertilized egg begins to get its early nutrition and to develop.

Sex of the Fetus

The sex of the baby is determined by its father at conception. During fertilization, there is an exchange of genetic material that determines the physical characteristics of the baby. This material, or genes, is grouped and carried in structures called "chromosomes." Every adult, male and female, has 46 chromosomes in each cell—22 matched pairs and one set of sex chromosomes. The one exception to this rule is the sperm cells and ovum, which carry 23 single chromosomes.

Fertilization, then, restores the full complement of chromosomes. The chromosomes which determine sex are labelled X and Y. All eggs have X chromosomes exclusively, while sperm cells are equally divided between X and Y. If a sperm cell carrying an X chromosome fertilizes the ovum, this XX combination produces a female baby. An XY combination results in the development of a male baby. It is a pity that Henry VIII's wives did not have this scientific knowledge available during their lifetimes.

Although doctors now know how sex is determined, they still have not developed a method of predetermining sex at conception. As a father of four daughters, I know this firsthand. There is a theory that sex can be controlled by certain techniques, and while none of these techniques have been proved scientifically valid, they result in no harm for the adventuresome couple who might want to try them. The theory suggests that X, or female-producing sperm cells, swim faster and live longer than the Y, or male-producing sperm.

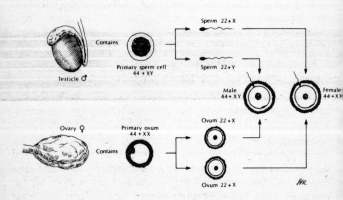

Male or female: Combination of a sperm with Y chromosome and ovum with X chromosome produces a male. The combination of sperm with X chromosome and ovum with X chromosome produces a female.

For a Boy

1. Your husband should abstain from intercourse for the five days preceding ovulation.
2. You should have intercourse on the day of ovulation.
3. Your husband should try for deep penetration at his orgasm.
4. You should douche directly before intercourse, using a solution of two tablespoons of baking soda to each quart of warm water.

For a Girl

1. You should cease intercourse two to three days before ovulation and not resume until two to three days after ovulation has occurred.
2. You should douche with an acidic solution of two tablespoons of white vinegar per quart of warm water prior to intercourse.
3. You should avoid orgasm.
4. Your husband should try for shallow penetration at orgasm.

Good luck! It may not work, but it will be fun trying.

THE LENGTH OF PREGNANCY

The average pregnancy lasts about 280 days, or 40 weeks, or 10 lunar months from the first day of the last menstrual period. Since about 14 days pass between the first day of menstruation and the day of ovulation, the fetus grows for about 266 days. The customary way to estimate the expected date of delivery is to count back three months from the first day of your last menstrual period and add seven days. If, for instance, your last menstrual period began June 10, your expected date of delivery would be March 17. But less than five percent of all pregnant women actually go into labor on the estimated date. About one-third deliver within five days of that date. The vast majority will give birth within two weeks of the due date. Since most calculations are based on the average 28-day cycle, ask your doctor for a special calculation if you menstruate more or less frequently.

While a good deal of confusion surrounds the dating of

pregnancy, it is necessary. Doctors like to have an accurate way of determining the age of the fetus to know what treatments are safe to give the mother if one should prove necessary during pregnancy. Mothers-to-be like to have an accurate way of knowing how far they have progressed in pregnancy and how much longer they will have to wait. Medical-legal experts are also interested in the length of pregnancy in cases where a child is born to a woman whose husband has been away for ten or more months, which puts the child's legitimacy in question. English law says a child is legitimate if born within 331 days of a husband's departure for war. The French have recognized the legitimacy of a child born 330 days after the death of a husband. A United States court accepted as legitimate a pregnancy which ended 355 days after the departure of the husband.

More accurate methods for dating pregnancies have been developed recently. These methods will be discussed in detail in the chapter on pregnancy diagnosis. They consist of the identification of fetal heart action by either hearing the fetal heart with an ultrasound fetoscope or by seeing the fetal heart beating by use of a sonogram. Both can occur at eight weeks of gestation. The use of serial fetal measurements by sonogram is the most accurate way of dating a pregnancy.

CHRONOLOGICAL DEVELOPMENT OF PREGNANCY

First Four Weeks

Days 1 to 4—menstruation.

Day 14—ovulation, followed by fertilization.

Days 14 to 20—migration of the fertilized egg through the Fallopian tube into the uterine cavity.

Days 20 to 21—implantation of the fertilized egg into the uterine wall.

Days 21 to 28—rapid growth of the fertilized egg and the development of an early placenta, the life-support system that provides food and oxygen for the fetus and takes away urine and carbon dioxide, the waste products of metabolism.

At the end of the first month of pregnancy, the fertilized egg is about 14 days old and is smaller than a BB shot.

The placenta is producing a hormone called "chorionic gonadotropin," which allows the mother's body to make a multitude of changes to support pregnancy. This hormone will now show up in the mother's blood so that a laboratory test at this time would confirm a suspicion of pregnancy.

Six Weeks

The fertilized egg with its nutritive material is about the size of a marble, but the developing baby is only half that size. Yet in the four weeks of growth since fertilization, it has developed a complete circulatory system and placenta. Its embryonic heart has begun to beat, and it has the beginnings of a real heart, brains, limbs, ears, nose, and eyes. The uterus is continuing to develop muscles and elastic tissue to support the fetus.

At this time, the presence of sufficient quantities of chorionic gonadotropin in the mother's urine allows the diagnosis of pregnancy to be made by a single two-minute home pregnancy test kit.

Eight Weeks (Two Lunar Months)

The ovum is about the size of a hen's egg; the developing embryo is slightly larger than the yolk. It has developed limbs and external genitalia. The cavity within the placenta is enlarging to accommodate fetal growth and already contains the amniotic fluid in which the fetus floats. The uterus also continues to grow and begins intermittent contractions, called "Braxton-Hicks contractions," which continue through pregnancy. The fetal heart can be heard by ultrasound fetoscope and seen beating by sonogram.

Twelve Weeks (Three Lunar Months)

The ovum is the size of a tennis ball, while the fetus itself is about two-thirds that size. In this third month of growth, the fetus has developed fingers, toes, and nails and continues to mature. The presence of twins can be accurately diagnosed by sonography at this time.

Sixteen Weeks (Four Lunar Months)

The fetus is about seven inches long and weighs about one-fifth of a pound. It has begun breathing movements and

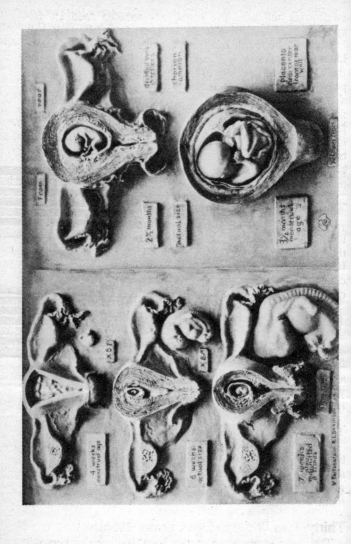

The development of pregnancy. *Courtesy Maternity Center Association, New York City.*

swallowing reflexes. The uterus has rounded suddenly because of a large increase in the amount of amniotic fluid.

Between the fourth and fifth months, the fetal movements, known as "quickening," can be felt by the mother. At first, the movements are very slight and may resemble mild gas pains. Eventually, there is no mistaking them. X-rays of the abdomen would show fetal bones. Your doctor may be listening now for the heartbeat with a simple stethoscope designed for this purpose. When he finishes, ask him to let you listen to the faint, rhythmic thump. Both movement and heartbeat become stronger as pregnancy progresses. Amniocentesis for genetic diagnosis can be performed at this time because of the accumulation of approximately a pint of fluid.

Twenty Weeks (Five Lunar Months)

The fetus is ten inches long and weighs a little more than half a pound. Its body is covered with a cheesy white protective material called "vernix caseosa." The facial features are fully developed, though the face is wrinkled and shriveled, causing the baby to look like a little old man. Early toenails can be seen.

Twenty-Four Weeks (Six Lunar Months)

The fetus is about 13 inches long and weighs about one and a half pounds. If born at this time, it might possibly survive a few hours, although the lungs are usually too immature to sustain life. Its skin is shiny and red and is covered all over with a fine hair known as "lanugo." Parts of the fetus can be felt by the doctor by feeling the abdomen.

Twenty-Eight Weeks (Seven Lunar Months)

The fetus is 15 inches long and weighs about two and a half pounds. Each day from this point on, its chances of surviving premature birth are better and better. The baby is getting larger and may be moving less because he has less room. Eyes open now and good hair development occurs.

Thirty-Two Weeks (Eight Lunar Months)

The fetus is about 16 inches long and weighs approximately three pounds. Its chances for survival are increased, despite the popular fallacy that seven-month babies live, but eight-month babies do not. Sheer poppycock! The closer the mother is to term, the better the baby's chance for survival.

Thirty-Six Weeks (Nine Lunar Months)

The baby is fully formed, measures 18 inches, weighs a little more than five pounds, and spends all his time maturing and building up fat tissue to provide him with warmth after birth.

Term

The baby is ready and waiting for some unknown signal that will precipitate labor. It measures about 19 inches and weighs an average of seven pounds.

PREMATURITY

A fully formed baby who weighs between two and five and a half pounds at birth is called a "premature" or "low-birth-weight" baby. The weight of the baby at birth is influenced by many factors, such as maternal nutrition, fetal disease, and racial factors. But the most common cause of prematurity (low birth weight) is birth before term.

Low-birth-weight babies are a particular concern to doctors because their life-support organs, especially their lungs, are usually not mature enough to allow the baby to live apart from the mother. The immature infant also has a greater chance of contracting infection.

Although premature infants comprise five to ten percent of all live births, the cause of most premature labors is not really known. Fifty to sixty percent of all premature births occur without a specific cause. Multiple pregnancies account for about twelve percent of all premature deliveries. The remainder of the cases can be attributed to maternal complications during pregnancy. Some conditions that predispose to early labor are premature rupture of the amniotic fluid; incompetency of the cervix; uterine growth defects; and serious maternal diseases such as kidney infections and pneumonia.

Modern medical technology has increased tremendously

Term-size fetus just before onset of labor, in fetal position within uterus. *Courtesy Maternity Center Association, New York City.*

the survival rate for the premature infant. One rule of thumb generally holds—the nearer to term, the greater the chance of survival. But if the mother's diet has been adequate and her physical condition good, the low-birth-weight infant has every chance of survival. Recently, various medications have been utilized to stop premature labor. They include beta-mimetics, alcohol, progesterone, narcotics, and sedatives. One drug, Ritodrine, has been approved by the FDA for this use. Recent experience has demonstrated its value in delaying labor in selected cases for a number of weeks (see chapter on pre-term labor).

POSTMATURITY

Consider the anguish of the poor expectant mother who waited patiently for her due date, only to pass it by one, two, or three weeks without giving birth. Her neighbors, friends, and relatives ask, "What! You're still around?" which sends her running to her doctor with the plea of "do something!"

Approximately four percent of all labors are delayed for three or more weeks past the estimated date of delivery. While this phenomenon causes great consternation in the family, doctors usually find no medical cause for concern in postmaturity pregnancies. This is true for mother and fetus alike. Women who do pass term should be carefully watched, however. Occasionally, a postmature infant developes placental insufficiency syndrome, which causes the fetus and placenta to lose weight and causes a decrease in the amount of amniotic fluid. Your doctor will usually monitor your pregnancy with tests if it appears you will significantly pass your due date. Some of these tests include the NST (nonstress test) fetal monitoring test, the estriol blood measurement, and sonographic study of the fetus. They are discussed in detail in Chapter 6.

In most cases, the presumed post-term baby really results from a miscalculated due date. Doctors do not routinely induce labor in the cases of postmature pregnancy for just this reason. But if there is no question of the accuracy of the menstrual history, and if the cervix—the mouth of the uterus—

is ready for birth, the doctor may induce labor by the use of a hormone called oxytocin or Pitocin. Cesarean section for postmature pregnancy is considered only under extremely unusual circumstances.

2
CHANGES CAUSED BY PREGNANCY

Pregnancy causes myriad changes in the mother, whose body is functioning like a highly efficient factory for the period of gestation. There are changes in every system of the body—some visible, others hidden within. Pregnancy is also accompanied by mood changes; some women feel exhilarated, and others depressed and irritable. In short, pregnancy is a highly individual experience. And each pregnancy for the same woman may be different also. But there are enough similarities in physical and psychological changes during gestation to classify them. I think that doing so will help you and your husband to understand some of what is happening during the nine-month preparation for birth.

GENERAL CHANGES

Weight Changes

Prompted by hormonal secretions, the whole body metabolism of the pregnant woman changes to accommodate her continued good health while she nourishes the fetus. The altered metabolism results in an increased efficiency of the body in squeezing out every bit of nutritive value foods have to offer. This handy change in body workings allows the mother to fulfill the health needs of herself and her developing baby without eating for two (see Chapter 5), but it can result in a slight acquisition of body fat on the mother.

Generally speaking, however, most of the weight gain of pregnancy is caused by the growing fetus and all its supporting systems. Statistics show that two-thirds of all normal women gain between 13 and 35 pounds during pregnancy. The average weight gain is two and a half pounds during the first three months, 10.8 pounds the second three months, and 11.2 pounds the last three months, which adds up to an average of 24.5 pounds. A gain of about one pound per week is suggested as a realistic maximum during the last half of pregnancy. More rigorous weight restriction than this is not justified and may be harmful, except under a doctor's orders and close supervision. At the same time, too much weight gain during pregnancy increases the possibility of complications and makes weight reduction after delivery much more difficult. Maintaining a balance will be discussed in more detail in Chapter 5, which deals with nutrition in pregnancy.

But just as a guide, a mother giving birth to a seven-and-a-half-pound baby can comfortably account for and lose twenty-four pounds: the weight of the infant, one pound for the placenta, a pound and a half of amniotic fluid, three pounds for increases in breast weight, two and a half pounds for the uterus. The remaining eight and a half pounds are attributable to protein and fat storage, water retention, and increased blood volume.

Fluid Retention

There is a general increase of about three pounds of body fluid in pregnancy. Most of this accumulation occurs toward the end of gestation and is often confused with swelling of the legs and ankles. This latter type of swelling is caused by pressure on the veins of the mother's legs from the fetus, placenta, and amniotic fluid.

Generalized water retention is caused by the increased circulatory needs of the mother, who is carrying the food and waste products in her blood for herself and her baby. The placenta helps by secreting sodium-retaining hormones, which chemically accentuate fluid accumulation. Doctors are not able to measure this retention directly, but they see it in swollen fingers, faces, and by weight gain that cannot be accounted for by fetal growth alone. The finger swelling causes many women to abandon their wedding rings toward the end of the pregnancy, much to the chagrin of fathers-to-be.

Skeletal System

One of the most common characteristics acquired in pregnancy is the duck-like strut of the expectant mother. While many women are able to maintain graceful posture throughout gestation, they are rather remarkable. Because of the increased prominence of the uterus and abdomen, the expectant mother tends to throw back her head and shoulders, exaggerating the curve of the small of the back and changing the body contour generally. In women carrying a very large baby or twins, this change of posture may be even more pronounced. The new posture may result in backache and strain in certain muscles (see Chapter 4).

Skin

The skin is affected by pregnancy in many ways. The skin covering organs directly affected by pregnancy, such as the nipples and the lips of the vagina (called the "vulva"), take on a darker hue. A thin, dark line forms up the middle of the abdomen. This line is known as the "linea nigra" and usually disappears within six months of delivery. The rapid growth of the fetus may cause layers of skin to be torn in the abdomen and on the breasts, upper thighs, and buttocks. These purplish-red zigzag marks are known as "straie gravidarum," or "stretch marks." Although there are many commercial preparations which claim to prevent these marks from forming, none has been found beneficial; either you get stretch marks, or you do not. Nothing will prevent their forming if your skin lacks elasticity. While they may be a little unsightly just following delivery, they usually lighten to near invisibility within several months.

Pigment in the face changes, too. The forehead, cheeks, and nose are often covered with brownish stains, which together are known as the "mask of pregnancy." Complexion is affected by changes in hormonal balance. Some women report acne. Others say their skin has never been so clear.

CHANGES IN THE ORGANS OF REPRODUCTION

The Uterus

Throughout pregnancy, the uterus, or womb, is enlarging to make room for the unborn fetus. Before conception, the uterus is the size and shape of a small pear and weighs about one and a half ounces. At the end of pregnancy, it weighs one and a half pounds. Its muscle fibers lengthen more than 100 times to support the developing baby. Uterine blood supply also increases to the point where veins carrying blood away from the uterus almost double their capacity.

There are two main parts to this primary organ of pregnancy. Its upper portion, called the "corpus," is very muscular and expansive. The uterine mouth, called the "cervix," is relatively inactive during fetal growth and development. But, at the time of birth, both sections work in harmony and help deliver the baby.

The uterus is shaped so that the baby's head will probably settle near the cervix, with its feet and buttocks in the upper portion of the corpus, the fundus. During the labor, the fundus begins contracting, pushing the baby down. The cervix, meanwhile, dilates to allow the baby's exit.

The Uterine Cervix

The cervix is the entrance and exit to the womb. Throughout pregnancy, the inch-and-a-half-long "door" stays closely shut and sealed with a plug of mucus to keep germs away from the developing baby. For this whole period, the cervix is soft and thick and passive. Then, just before labor, it begins a thinning or effacement until the whole length of the cervix disappears and the entire cervix is only a fraction of an inch thick. As labor progresses, the cervix opens or dilates to about the width of the hand to allow the baby to pass through. This dilation is coordinated with the contracting movement of the uterus.

Sometimes, the cervix fails to dilate, which may necessitate Cesarean delivery. Once in a great while, the cervix fails to stay closed, a condition known as "cervical incompetence." This is a rare cause of late abortion. The condition can be remedied by running a string or suture around the perimeter of the opening of the cervix which is then drawn and tied like a lace until labor begins, when it is removed.

Position of the Uterus

The position of the uterus is a key factor in determining the length and progress of pregnancy. For the first two months, it is situated below the pelvic bones and cannot be felt from the outside, but as it enlarges it moves forward and lies on the bladder, causing more frequent urination than normal. As it enlarges, it rises out of the pelvis and in time lies against the abdominal wall, where the doctor's trained hand can feel it externally. It continues to move up until it has displaced the intestines and stomach, which sometimes causes indigestion.

Each stage of growth of the uterus is accompanied by abdominal landmarks which help the doctor estimate the length of pregnancy. If the uterus is one-quarter of the way to the navel, you are two months pregnant; if it is halfway between the pubic bone and the navel, you are three months; three-quarters of the way marks four months of fetal growth. A uterus reaches the navel at about the fifth month of pregnancy. The uterus then rises one-quarter of the way from the navel to the end of the rib cage each month. Just before term, it sinks back to the eight-month level. This method of determining the length of pregnancy is called "Bartholomew's Rule" and is really an approximation because of many variables in measuring, such as the thickness of the uterine wall, the amount of amniotic fluid, the size of the baby, or the presence of twins. But it is a fairly accurate and helpful tool for the doctor in confirming his original estimation of the date of delivery.

Lightening

About two weeks before birth, the uterus sinks. This sinking is caused by the moving of the head down into the pelvic cavity. It is called "dropping" or "settling" or "lightening," and it occurs in about 65 percent of all pregnancies prior to labor although it is more common in women having a first baby.

Lightening may occur suddenly or gradually; in fact, it may occur without your even knowing it. It allows you to

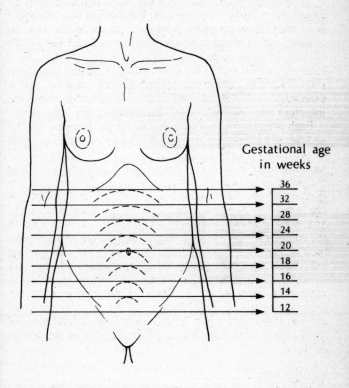

Gestational age
in weeks

36
32
28
24
20
18
16
14
12

This figure illustrates the height of the top of the uterus during the various weeks of pregnancy. Note that the uterus can first be felt abdominally at 12 weeks and is at the level of the navel at 20 weeks.

digest food more easily, to breathe a little easier. Your clothes will probably fit better, too. But because of the lowered position of the uterus, the early pressure symptoms of constipation and frequent urination may return. Yet lightening is usually a welcome sign because it means that the head is not too large to go through the pelvis and that delivery is not too far away.

Vagina and Vulva

For the purpose of reproduction, the vagina serves as the birth channel. Like the cervix, it stays relatively passive through the pregnancy, waiting to perform its special function at birth.

In preparation for birth, the veins enlarge enormously almost from the time of implantation, so that the vagina and its lips, the vulva, take on a deep port color. This purplish hue is known as "Chadwick's sign of pregnancy." The vein engorgement may make intercourse a little uncomfortable, since the capacity of the vagina is diminished by the enlarged veins.

You may notice an increase in vaginal discharge, caused by the increased blood supply or by secretions from the cervix. If this discharge burns or has a disagreeable odor, report it to your doctor.

During pregnancy, the vagina stretches in length and increases in elasticity, so that at birth it can accommodate the body of a baby comfortably; then it shrinks back to its original size. Because the mouth of the vagina is not as elastic as the rest, it is common obstetrical practice in this country to slit the opening of the vagina to accommodate the baby's exit and prevent unnecessary tearing. This incision is called "episiotomy" and necessitates the "stitches" associated with delivery.

Abdomen

The greatest bodily change of all takes place in the abdomen. As the baby grows, you suddenly develop a great configuration that you may not be able to see over or lie on. Your navel may pop out, making it visible through thin layers of clothing. Stretch marks may develop, too.

The stretching of the abdomen is made possible by the

relaxation of the inner wall, especially in the area around the navel. It often seems impossible to a fat-stomached woman that her abdomen can stretch to cover the baby. It always does. In first pregnancies, the wall is very tense, so that sometimes the baby grows faster than the uterine and abdominal walls can stretch, and the mother may periodically experience a tight feeling in the abdomen. For women who have had many babies, the abdomen may begin to droop, making it look very much like a sagging breast.

Breasts

Beginning in the second month of pregnancy, when the mammary or milk-producing glands begin to develop, the breasts grow, pleasing fathers and mothers alike. This growth, like most, continues throughout the period of gestation, reaching maximum potential during lactation. The breasts also become softer. Their veins enlarge and show up as bluish streaks. Striae gravidarum, the stretch marks, may also be present.

During pregnancy, the nipples are more erect, and the aureola, the darker pigmentation surrounding them, may become even more deeply pigmented. Fluid may ooze out of the breasts quite early. In later months, this fluid changes to a diluted premilk called "colostrum." This yellowish fluid nourishes the baby for the few days after birth before milk comes into the breasts of the nursing mother. Most doctors believe that colostrum is beneficial in that it contains most of the mother's resistance to disease antibodies and offers the child of the nursing mother equal immunity for the first few months of life. However, some feel that this factor is relatively unimportant since the majority of the antibodies are obtained while the infant is still in the uterus.

Ovaries

The ovaries, which produced the egg that was fertilized, play a different role during the pregnancy itself. One ovary usually becomes enlarged and grows a cyst or fluid-containing structure called a "corpus luteum." The cyst secretes hormones that signal the mother's body to prepare for gestation. The corpus luteum is the site at which the egg has broken away from the ovary during ovulation. It continues secreting hormones for six weeks until the placenta is formed to take over the task.

PSYCHOLOGICAL CONSIDERATIONS IN PREGNANCY

Every woman brings to pregnancy her own individual character and outlook, each of which is a product of inherited, environmental, and cultural factors. Real and imagined hazards, inadequate education, personal immaturity, or previous experiences may cause some expectant mothers real anxiety. My personal observation is, however, that women who take the time to read about pregnancy and childbirth and who take it as a natural occurrence of life are much more relaxed about the whole process.

Most anxieties of pregnancy are caused by one or more of the following factors:

1. Fear of pain and/or death.
2. Taboos regarding reproductive functions.
3. Ambivalent feelings about children.
4. Inability to accept the responsibility of motherhood.
5. Distortions of the body, resulting in the feeling that beauty and femininity are lost.

Women, with the aid of their physicians, can usually work out these potential problems during their antepartum period. With the knowledge gained through understanding and education, fear of pain and death can be easily dismissed. Superstitions are also easily cast aside if discussed rationally. Most of the ambivalent feelings toward pregnancy can be resolved when dealt with, and women should understand that any bodily changes are only temporary.

Your physician and your husband can be most helpful if you find pregnancy is getting you down momentarily. Your doctor can refute superstitions with fact. The expectant father or other family members can provide comfort during periods of distress.

Ironically, the factors which cause fear and anxiety in some women are sources of motivation and strength in more confi-dent mothers-to-be.

Many expectant fathers are equally fearful of pregnancy. Since the event does not affect them as directly as it does the mother, they may not at first seem so enthusiastic as their wives would like. Education of fathers-to-be helps here, too.

But remember that the nine-month period is as much for the parents as it is for the baby. No matter how much a child is wanted, or how much education the parents have about childbirth, they still need time to get used to the idea of being parents.

3
THE DIAGNOSIS
OF PREGNANCY

For most women, a missed menstrual period signifies pregnancy. Most women whose period is two or more weeks late assume they are pregnant, especially if they have engaged in unprotected intercourse within the past month. The doctor, however, looks at many more factors before positively diagnosing pregnancy. Using the patient's perceptions, his observations, and some more objective measures, such as laboratory tests, he pieces together information taken from many systems of the body before concluding a woman is pregnant.

For the purposes of diagnosis and monitoring, pregnancy is divided into three three-month segments called "trimesters," each of which has characteristic signs.

FIRST TRIMESTER

Patient's Perceptions

1. *Cessation of menstruation*—This is one of the most important symptoms of pregnancy, but it must occur in a woman who has previously been regular to be of any real value. It is reasonably safe to assume that a woman who menstruates normally is not pregnant, and that one who can conceive and suddenly ceases to menstruate

probably is pregnant. The absence of a menstrual period is only presumptive evidence, but it is useful, of course, in fixing the date of conception and, therefore, determining the probable time of labor. Vaginal bleeding which is indistinguishable from menstruation can continue following conception. It is not rare for a woman to have one or two periods after she is pregnant, but usually this type of vaginal bleeding is less profuse than that associated with menses. Other conditions which can delay menstruation other than pregnancy are changes in climate and environment, external influences, severe illness, menopause, and lactation. Another common cause is the recent use of contraceptive pills.

2. *Nausea and vomiting*—Missed menses accompanied by nausea and vomiting are highly suspicious signs of pregnancy. About half of all pregnant women experience these symptoms in the early part of pregnancy. They may appear as early as the second week of pregnancy, but they usually begin in the fifth week. Most women awaken feeling nauseous and find the feeling disappears after breakfast. Others become sick to their stomachs at the slightest smell of food (see Chapter 4).

3. *Increased frequency of urination*—Because of the pressure of the growing uterus in early fetal formation, the pregnant woman will probably need to urinate more frequently. This is an early presumptive symptom and is seriously considered only with those mentioned earlier (see Chapter 4).

4. *Vaginal discharge*—Throughout pregnancy, vaginal secretions change. They get thicker, whiter, and stickier. This change is noticeable soon after a missed period and is a corroborating bit of evidence to an already well-established case.

More Objective Signs

1. *Body changes*—More conclusive evidence of pregnancy are the body changes, some of which can be seen almost immediately following conception. The breasts become enlarged, sore, and tingling as early as the

fourth week of pregnancy. Bluish discoloration of the vulva and vagina may be observed, as discussed in the previous chapter. Softening of the cervix and vagina may also occur early in gestation, along with a softening of the lower part of the uterus. This uterine change, called "Hagar's sign," may be observed by the examining doctor as early as the sixth week of pregnancy. While performing the examination, the doctor looks for other changes in the uterus, such as enlargement and shift in position, all of which are highly suspicious of pregnancy when considered together.

2. *Basal body temperature*—The basal body temperature is of great help in early confirmation of pregnancy. The basal body temperature is a measure of body heat taken upon waking, before getting out of bed. The body's normal basal temperature is below 98°F. After ovulation, however, it usually rises to above 98°F, where it stays until menstruation, at which time it returns to its lower level. If a woman has conceived, her temperature remains at the higher reading. Since ovulation usually occurs 14 days before the end of the menstrual cycle, a sustained reading of above 98°F for more than 16 days following ovulation is highly suggestive of pregnancy. The diagnosis of pregnancy based on a high basal body temperature has been shown to be correct 97 percent of the time.

3. *Biological tests for pregnancy*—Pregnancy can now be confirmed in laboratory tests about ten days after conception. In 1929, Ascheim and Zondek, two endocrinologists, found that the urine and blood of an expectant mother contained hormones related to pregnancy. They concluded that diagnosis of pregnancy could be made by confirming the presence of those hormones. Through the years, these tests consisted of injecting the urine or blood specimen into a laboratory animal and watching for changes in their sexual organs. These tests took days and were not extremely reliable. Today, however, doctors use chemicals to test for a specific hormone, chorionic gonadotropin, which is produced by the placenta, an organ specifically formed for pregnancy.

New tests are now available for the testing of maternal blood specimens that use a technique called radioimmunoassay. These tests are so sensitive that they can pick up levels of chorionic gonadotropin (specific for pregnancy) as early as 9 to 10 days after conception. In other words, pregnancy can be diagnosed even before a menstrual period is missed.

Most women and their physicians will not utilize these sensitive tests on a routine basis but will wait for a missed menstrual period. However, these tests are valuable in certain instances of problem pregnancies such as women with habitual abortions and possible ectopic pregnancies.

The urine tests for pregnancy have also been developed for greater sensitivity and simplicity. There are many kits available over the counter for home pregnancy testing. These tests are usually not positive until 10 to 14 days after a missed period or four weeks after conception.

I advise every woman who has a positive home screening test be checked by a physician for confirmation.

Ultrasound Tests for Pregnancy

The fetal heart starts beating as early as 6 to 8 weeks of gestation. This definite sign of a *live* pregnancy can be diagnosed at about eight weeks by two methods: the use of a type of special stethoscope that uses the Doppler ultrasound principle to pick up the beating heart; sonography and especially real-time ultrasound can visualize the beating heart (or hearts for that matter) within the fetal sac as early as eight weeks. Ultrasound will be discussed in detail in Chapter 6.

These techniques are very valuable for diagnosing a *live* pregnancy early and their repeated use are especially helpful in problem pregnancies.

SECOND TRIMESTER

If a diagnosis of pregnancy has not been made by the end of the first trimester (which is highly unlikely), new signs appear that should cause you to seek medical advice to find out what is happening. If a diagnosis has been made, the doctor will still watch for symptoms as an indication to him that the pregnancy is progressing smoothly and that the baby is continuing to grow.

1. *Abdominal size*—If it has not happened earlier, by the beginning of the fourth lunar month of pregnancy, the abdomen should begin to protrude. This protrusion may come all of a sudden, following a rapid increase in the volume of amniotic fluid during the fourth month of gestation. You will not mistake the growing abdomen as an ordinary potbelly. The abdomen housing the fetus is low and very firm. It will probably be well hidden under loose-fitting clothes for the first few months of pregnancy, but will be very obvious when uncovered.

2. *Quickening*—Somewhere following the fourth month, you will feel a slight, indescribable sensation in the abdomen. At first, you will just make mental note of it, but within several weeks, the feeling will be quite pronounced and will resemble the fluttering of tiny birds' wings or the rising of bubbles along the wall of the uterus. These sensations are called "quickening," and they represent the first perceptions of fetal movement. The movement is felt earlier by women who have felt it before. Quickening is only of presumptive value to diagnosis, since intestinal movements or abdominal-muscle contraction can give the impression of fetal movement.

3. *Fetal movement*—Unlike quickening, which is basically an initial perception, persistent fetal movement is a very definite sign of pregnancy, which occasionally can be observed as early as the sixteenth week. If you look, you will be able to see a slight momentary bulge of the abdominal wall, or the passage of a limb across your stomach. Sometimes the movements are so vigorous that they are visible through clothing. If you or your husband lays one hand on your abdomen, you may feel a weak knock or stroke. This is a positive sign of fetal life.

4. *Uterine contractions*—Intermittent uterine contractions may be felt any time after the tenth week, and they may continue right up to the time of labor. The uterus is so

sensitive to touch that it can harden at the slightest pressure during the doctor's examination and will relax as quickly as the hand is removed. These contractions are a very reliable sign of pregnancy and are normal.

5. *Fetal heartbeat*—The fetal heart can be heard by a doctor using a regular fetoscope from the fourth to the fifth month on. The heart becomes stronger and louder as the child grows, until by the seventh month, your husband should be able to hear it by placing his ear on your abdomen (caution: a heavy head will be kicked). What he will hear is a fast ticktock, which sounds as if it were muffled by a pillow. The rate will range from 120 to 160 beats per minute, almost twice the pulse of the average adult; the fetus has a lot of work to do.

6. *Fetal structure*—By the end of the second trimester, the doctor should be able to feel several key parts of the fetus merely by feeling your abdomen. The head and back can be felt quite easily by the trained hand, and their presence would be confirmed by x-ray, if one were taken. To summarize then, pregnancy is diagnosed at varying points in gestation by the following signs:

Early:

1. Cessation of menses—presumptive symptom.
2. Nausea and vomiting—presumptive symptom.
3. Changes in the breasts—presumptive symptom.
4. Discoloration of the genitals, softening of the uterus (Chadwick's and Hagar's signs)—presumptive symptoms.
5. Softening of the vagina and cervix—presumptive symptom.
6. Changes in form, size, position, and consistency of the uterus—probable sign.
7. Positive laboratory test—98 percent certain.
8. Ultrasound hearing or seeing of fetal heart—100 percent certain.

Late:

1. Lack of menstruation—presumptive sign.
2. Quickening—presumptive sign.

3. Intermittent uterine contractions—probable sign.
4. Fetal movements—certain sign.
5. Feeling the fetus through the abdomen—certain sign.
6. Fetal heart tones—certain sign.
7. X-ray examination of the fetus—certain sign.

4
PRENATAL (ANTEPARTUM) CARE

Pregnancy and childbirth today are safer than most of the stresses of modern life. This generalization is true because of the great emphasis on prenatal care now given in this country. It is important that every woman visit a doctor as soon as pregnancy is suspected. This visit will mark the formal beginning of prenatal, or antepartum, care. The purpose of prenatal care is to ensure the delivery of a healthy baby to a healthy mother.

The fetus throughout pregnancy is not totally accessible to the doctor who wants to know its condition but cannot see it inside the safe, cushioned environment of the womb. He can, however, monitor the mother on a regular basis, looking for signs and symptoms which might indicate trouble. The doctor is especially sensitive to signs in the early months, when the developing human is most vulnerable to outside influences, such as medications taken by the mother.

Good prenatal care should really begin at conception. By the time pregnancy is usually confirmed, about six weeks following the last menstrual period, most of the fetal organs are already formed. Its circulatory system and major sense organs are well developed. Ideally, every woman should be completely examined before she plans to become pregnant.

31

Preconceptional care should include a complete medical, dental, and gynecologic examination. Testing for rubella (German measles) susceptibility by a blood test is also important. If rubella blood antibodies are not present, vaccination against rubella should be performed. However, it is very important not to become pregnant for three months following this vaccination.

Preconceptional genetic screening for Tay-Sachs disease has also recently become available. Jewish couples of Eastern European extraction have a higher risk of this genetic disorder. Screening for the carrier state should be done so that diagnostic amniocentesis can be performed during the pregnancy if both partners should be carriers (see fetal diagnosis chapter for further details).

But we do not live in a perfect world. You can pretty much rely on the skill of your physician to watch closely what will probably be a smooth and uneventful pregnancy.

Choosing the Doctor

You will probably have several choices of medical care for your pregnancy. Your family doctor may care for you and deliver your baby, or you may choose to go to one of the many fine hospital clinics which are available. But chances are, you will choose a doctor who specializes in obstetrics, that branch of medicine concerned with birth. An obstetrician is the physician whose primary concern is the management of pregnancy, labor and delivery, and postpartum care. In England, midwifery carries the same meaning as obstetrics does in the United States. As a matter of fact, in this country, there is a resurgence in the use of nurses trained as midwives, working directly with physicians to deliver babies. This medical team usually works at a family health center, which is another alternative to the private obstetrician for the management of pregnancy, one that will probably cost less. But if you are planning to use a private physician and have not yet chosen one, there are some facts you should have to make your choice.

Before 1930, there was an average of 60 maternal deaths for every 10,000 live births. Today, there is only about one maternal death per 10,000 births, and the vast majority of these women enter pregnancy with a previous disease. This overall reduction is a superb testament to the increased quality of obstetrical care. Many factors are responsible for the reduction, including the development of antibiotics to fight infection. But the most important factor is probably increased education and training in the field of obstetrics.

The American Board of Obstetrics and Gynecology, which certifies specialists in the field, has very high standards. A doctor seeking certification must be a graduate of an accredited medical school and must thereafter complete one year's internship and three years' residency in an accredited hospital. After that, he must practice in his specialty for several years and then pass both written and oral examinations.

If no one can recommend an acceptable physician to you, contact your local medical society and ask who among its members are board-certified obstetricians. Or you can write to the American Board of Obstetrics and Gynecology for a list of members in your immediate area. Recently, a superspecialist in obstetrics, called a perinatologist, has evolved. These experts are usually associated with major medical centers and offer consultation in high-risk obstetrical cases.

The First Visit

When you first visit the doctor, you will probably be anxious for him or her to examine you to confirm your suspicion that you are going to have a baby. Or, if pregnancy has been confirmed, you will want the doctor to give you some instructions to follow during this very special period of gestation. But before that, the doctor will probably want a complete medical history of you and your family. He or she will pay particular attention to your past obstetrical history, which includes a brief account of each former pregnancy and delivery, miscarriages, or abortions. You will also be asked about the history of any herpes infections.

With this completed, you will be given a physical examination, starting with a measure of your blood pressure, which will be checked at each succeeding visit. An abnormal rise in blood pressure late in pregnancy may indicate the development of toxemia, a disturbance in the system which can occur only in pregnancy.

You will be weighed, and your doctor will use your weight

at this visit as a reference point to know how much you are gaining and how quickly you are doing so.

The doctor will take a blood sample, which will give many facts. First, he or she will measure the hemoglobin, the oxygen-carrying protein of red blood cells. Too few red cells will indicate anemia, which is very common among pregnant women. If you have anemia in pregnancy, chances are you will tire more easily and will not be able to support your own health and the growth of the fetus as well as you might otherwise. This condition is easily corrected by daily supplements of iron. The doctor may give you a prescription for iron, in addition to one for prenatal vitamins. From the same blood sample, the doctor will determine your blood type, especially your Rh status, which is discussed at length in Chapter 6. He or she will also do a blood test to rule out syphilis, a venereal disease which can cause congenital abnormalities in the fetus. Other blood tests commonly being performed include testing for susceptibility to rubella, toxoplasmosis, and the presence of abnormal blood antibodies.

You will probably be asked by the doctor to bring a specimen of your first voided urine on the day of your visit, and you will be asked to do so for each visit thereafter. By analyzing the specimen, the doctor can check for the presence of sugar or protein, which would indicate diabetes or kidney abnormalities respectively.

The doctor will also examine you on the table. A vaginal examination will be done, which will also give a great deal of information. By feeling the uterus, the doctor can measure its size, which will confirm pregnancy. The birth channel will be measured to see if it is wide enough to allow the passage of a baby. Ask for a Papanicolaou smear, the cancer-screening test which every woman should have at least once a year. The doctor may take another smear to test for gonorrhea, a venereal disease. (In the early 1970's, gonorrhea was the most commonly reported communicable disease in the country after the common cold, with an estimated two million new cases every year.)

While are you on the table, your doctor will examine your breasts and feel your abdomen for growth of the uterus. The uterus with the fetus within can usually be felt through the abdomen after the third month of pregnancy.

After the physical is complete, the doctor will outline the course of pregnancy and ask you to return every three to four weeks until the eighth month, when you will probably visit the doctor every two weeks. In the ninth month, you will go every week and sometimes more often.

On most of these visits, the doctor will take your blood pressure and weight and will analyze your urine sample. Fetal growth will be measured by feeling the abdomen, but occasionally a vaginal examination may also be performed to monitor fetal growth, position, and size more closely. Vaginal examinations during the ninth month are routine procedure for many physicians to determine if the baby's head will pass through the pelvic cavity and to determine the condition of the cervix to predict the possible onset of labor. Sometimes this examination is followed by some slight vaginal bleeding which should be no cause for worry.

Instructions to patients vary from doctor to doctor, but basically the diet, sleep, bowel function, clothing, bathing, and dental care are reviewed. The major goals of this first examination are to check the health of the mother and fetus; to determine the age of the pregnancy and fetus; and to start a plan for continuing obstetrical care.

Don't be afraid to ask questions. The more you know, the less frightened you will be and the more you will enjoy your pregnancy. Certain warning symptoms may also be outlined. If any of these are present, they should be reported to the doctor immediately. Smoking, drug, and alcohol use will also be discussed.

Potential Danger Symptoms of Pregnancy

1. *Vaginal bleeding*—Most vaginal bleeding is probably insignificant, since 20 percent of all pregnant women report having it in some form during the first three months of gestation. Bleeding is caused by a leaking blood vessel or a number of other factors. But it may also be a sign of impending miscarriage. Always report this to your doctor.
2. *Swelling of the face or fingers*—Swelling or bloating of the face and fingers may be a sign of fluid retention, but it may also signal the onset of toxemia, and it, too, should be reported to the doctor immediately.

3. *Blurring of vision*—Like swelling, blurred vision may be a sign of fluid retention or of toxemia.

4. *Severe and continuous headaches*—These may result from rhinitis, a sinus condition often occurring in pregnancy, but they can also mean that an excessive amount of fluid is being retained or that toxemia is developing. Therefore, they should be reported to your doctor.

5. *Severe pain in the abdomen*—The abdomen during pregnancy may be a little sore from the rapid growth of the fetus. Intermittent contractions may also be normal. But constant or debilitating pain is not normal and should not go unattended.

6. *Persistent vomiting*—Some nausea and vomiting occur in 50 percent of all pregnancies and by itself should be no cause for alarm. But persistent vomiting should be reported to your doctor.

7. *Fever*—Fever usually means that there is a foreign virus or bacteria in the body to which your system is reacting. Fever in pregnancy is no exception. A high temperature may result from a cold, but it may also mean an infection in the reproductive or urinary tract, so it should be reported immediately.

8. *Fluid discharge from the vagina*—Vaginal discharge during pregnancy usually increases, becoming thick and sticky. A clear fluid discharge is not so normal. It may be just a secretion of the cervix, but it may also indicate a leakage of amniotic fluid, which means there is a rupture in the chorion, the membrane surrounding the fetus and fluid.

Summary of the Danger Signs of Pregnancy

1. Vaginal bleeding.
2. Swelling of the face or fingers.
3. Blurring of vision.
4. Severe and continuous headaches.
5. Severe pain in the abdomen.
6. Persistent vomiting.
7. Fever.
8. Fluid discharge from the vagina.

GENERAL HYGIENE OF THE MOTHER

1. *Exercise*—Pregnant women tire more easily and, therefore, require more rest to prevent fatigue. Vigorous activity, such as driving or riding in a car over very rough terrain, or skydiving should obviously be avoided. Sports such as golf, tennis, bowling, and horseback riding are usually permitted at a moderate or mild pace. The current enthusiasm for jogging has raised the question of its safety for pregnant women. Continuation of pre-pregnancy exercise habits, including jogging, is not harmful. In fact, several women have run in marathons of considerable distance without harm to themselves or the fetus. All these women, of course, were in excellent health and well conditioned for the event. These activities are usually best discussed on a personal basis with your physician.

   A certain amount of exercise is mandatory for the pregnant woman. The benefits derived from exercises are improved blood circulation, better appetite, more efficient digestion of food, and more restful sleep. Of course, women who are accustomed to exercise and sports can tolerate more exercise than those who lead a more sedentary life. Walking is an exercise that most women can and should do. Usually low-heeled—not flat—shoes are most comfortable and are best for back comfort.

2. *Employment*—Strenuous activity during pregnancy—activities that would subject the mother to severe physical strain—should obviously be avoided. No work or play should be extended to the point of exhaustion. In general, however, most types of female employment are well tolerated by the expectant mother and are usually encouraged. There have been arbitrary limits on employment of pregnant women set by some corporations and boards of education, which require the expectant mother to stop work two to three months before term. Many women, however, work right up to the moment labor begins. My wife, a practicing attorney, went into labor in the subway coming home from work. This is an extreme case, however.

3. *Travel*—Although there is much superstition surrounding the subject, there are no restrictions on travel during

pregnancy for most women. This would include travel by train, car, airplane, and boat. The chief drawback to travel is that skilled obstetrical care may not be available should trouble arise during a trip. Women with poor obstetrical histories should avoid unnecessary travel. Other than that, let your comfort be your guide.

4. *Bathing*—There is no objection to shower or sponge baths at any time during pregnancy or following delivery. The question of tub baths varies from doctor to doctor. In general, the old idea that tub water enters the vagina, thereby carrying infection into the uterus, is now believed to have little merit. I allow my patients to take tub baths any time during pregnancy but caution them about the possibility of slipping or falling in the bathtub. Of course, once the cervix starts to dilate or if there is any question of leakage of amniotic fluid, I ask the mother to stop tub baths. Recent evidence suggests that prolonged exposure to excessive heat in a sauna or hot tub may be harmful and caution is suggested.

5. *Hair care*—The care of the hair is no different in pregnancy. Some women, however, will notice a change in the amount of body their hair has and may want to condition it, since appearance has much to do with psychological health during pregnancy.

6. *Clothing*—Pregnancy today need not be the horror it was for fashionable women in the past. Maternity clothes today are very stylish. You should, however, remember to choose clothes that are loose enough to allow a little expansion and that are comfortable and do not bind. Shoes should be low-heeled, not flat, and large enough to allow for swelling in warm weather. Underwear can either help your comfort or hinder it terribly. Never wear circular garters around the upper legs, which would cut circulation and cause veins to swell. Backache or pressure symptoms caused by the enlarging uterus can be helped by a well-fitting maternity girdle. The enlarging breasts can be made more comfortable by wearing a supportive brassiere, not necessarily a maternity bra.

7. *Sexual intercourse*—There is general agreement that in a normal pregnancy—one without complications—sex is considered safe, and most couples can continue inter-

course with orgasm until shortly before birth. Certain positions, such as rear entry position for vaginal intercourse or female astride the male partner may be comfortable during the later months.

Misinformation about the effects of sex on pregnancy may make a couple unconsciously afraid that sex will harm the baby. Both partners may experience emotional and sexual changes during pregnancy. Some women find they have a lower sex drive, some greater, and some no change at all. Emotional as well as physical adjustments sometimes have to be made to continue your relationship during pregnancy.

Comfort is a good guide to sex during pregnancy; however, if threatened miscarriage, threatened premature labor, bleeding, or amniotic fluid leakage occurs, sex should be avoided. Women who have bad obstetrical histories may need special advice from their physicians.

8. *Douching*—Douching is also allowable during pregnancy if the douche bag is placed no more than two feet above the level of the hips to prevent strong fluid pressure. The nozzle of the douche set should not be inserted more than three inches into the vagina. However, the need for douching is rare.

9. *Smoking*—Even a moderate use of tobacco may have an adverse effect on the course of pregnancy. The use of tobacco has been correlated with the increased incidence of prematurity, small babies, and other complications of pregnancy. Cigarette smoking is hazardous to your health and should be avoided by women pregnant and nonpregnant.

10. *Alcohol consumption*—Women who drink excessive amounts of alcohol face a high risk of a child with multiple abnormalities. It is now known that even some moderate drinking may be harmful. Women who drink one to two ounces of pure alcohol (the equivalent of 2 to 4 beers, glasses of wine, or cocktails) per day have nearly a 10 percent risk of fetal abnormalities, and those who drink this amount twice per week have an increased risk of spontaneous abortion. We do not know what, if any, amount of alcohol is safe. Therefore, keep your drinking to a bare minimum.

11. *Medications*—Because certain drugs have been shown to cross the placenta and enter the baby's system, medication of any kind should not be routinely used in pregnancy. But if you have a headache or a cold, your doctor will be able to tell you what you can take to relieve discomfort (see Chapter 13). Women who are trying to conceive should also be careful about drugs since the exact time of conception will not be known.

12. *Immunizations*—The following table summarizes the recommendations of the American College of Obstetricians and Gynecologists over the safety of various immunization techniques during pregnancy:

  1. Tetanus-diptheria—Give if no primary series or no booster in 10 years.
  2. Polio—Not recommended routinely for adults.
  3. Mumps—Not safe.
  4. Rubella—Not safe.
  5. Typhoid—Recommended if traveling to high risk regions.
  6. Smallpox—No need, it has been eradicated.
  7. Yellow fever—Immunize only before travel in high risk areas.
  8. Cholera—Same.
  9. Hepatitis A—After exposure or before travel in developing countries.
  10. Rabies—Same as nonpregnant.
  11. Influenza—For pregnant women with serious underlying disease.

COMMON COMPLAINTS OF PREGNANCY

During the course of pregnancy, many women experience various aches and pains or more specific discomforts. These vary from person to person, and many women experience none at all. But if you do experience some, you should understand that you are not alone. Even more comforting is the knowledge that most of these annoyances are short-lived and pass with that stage of pregnancy.

1. *Backache*—Backache is one of the most common minor problems in pregnant women. It is caused by the changes

in posture required by the enlarging uterus and fetus, and discussed in Chapter 2. Minor backache that is *persistent* is usually best treated with local heat, analgesics, and occasionally the use of a back support or a maternity girdle. The exercises outlined in the chapter on Lamaze may also help alleviate backaches. Severe backache may be incapacitating and should be treated by your doctor.

2. *Bowel habits*—Constipation during pregnancy is very common. Decreased physical activity and the partial obstruction of the lower bowel by the growing fetus increase the tendency toward irregularity. The increasing weight of the baby and uterus may cause the lower bowel to develop hemorrhoids. These are swellings of the vein, which may be painful and may occasionally bleed.

Most women who have had fairly regular bowel habits before pregnancy may control the tendency toward constipation by (a) taking a sufficient quantity of fluid in the diet, (b) participating in a reasonable amount of activity, and (c) using natural laxatives, such as Milk of Magnesia, prune juice, and whole-bran cereals. Avoid the routine use of harsh laxatives and enemas because they may be habit-forming. Here again, your physician is your best guide.

3. *Excessive urination*—You may find yourself having to urinate more frequently as the baby grows, irritating the bladder in the process.

4. *Fatigue*—Pregnant women tire easily, especially in the first and third trimesters. You may find it necessary to retire a little earlier at night for a while or stretch out with your feet up at some point during the day. If you are a working woman, you might try bringing your lunch and resting on a lounge in the ladies' room during your lunch break. If this is a possibility, you will feel better.

5. *Swollen ankles and varicose veins*—Many women develop swelling in the extremities as the baby grows, putting pressure on the veins of the legs. Some women who have this problem also have the inherited tendency to get varicose veins. These are veins which are distended and swollen and may be painful and tender.

Swelling and varicose veins are aggravated by long periods of standing and by large weight gains by the mother.

Many women find elastic support hose put on before getting out of bed provide the best relief from the discomfort of varicose veins. Support stockings vary in strength from mildly elasticized hose to surgical stockings that require expert fitting. Your doctor is your best guide in choosing the proper stocking to be used.

Varicose veins are also treated by elevating the legs several times a day, maintaining normal weight gain and preventing fluid accumulation. Many of the changes in the veins regress following completion of the pregnancy.

6. *Heartburn*—Heartburn is one of the most common complaints of pregnancy. The growing fetus gives the stomach less room to expand, causing some regurgitation of food into the esophagus, the "food tube" that runs from the mouth to the stomach. Heartburn, then, is the irritation of the esophagus. This irritation often causes a burning sensation in the lower chest or midabdominal area. Treatment consists of taking antacid medication and eating bland food. Sodium bicarbonate should never be used, however, because the use of sodium tends to promote water retention. Sleeping on two or three pillows may also prove helpful.

7. *Headaches*—Headaches are a common complaint of early pregnancy. No cause has been demonstrated for them, however, and most disappear by midpregnancy. Treatment usually consists of simple analgesics, but check with your doctor to see what he prescribes.

8. *Nausea and vomiting*—Mild nausea and vomiting is one of the most common problems of the first trimester of pregnancy. About 50 percent of women have some degree of nausea, and a third have some vomiting. Severe nausea and vomiting has become uncommon.

Symptoms may appear as early as the second week of pregnancy, but they usually develop about the fifth week. They may continue to the third month or sometimes longer. Most women report feeling sick in the morning upon rising or after breakfast, and they vomit this meal. The nausea does not often recur during the remainder of the day. The cause of this nausea is not generally known, but various theories have been postulated to explain it. These include stomach spasm, hormone imbalance, blood-sugar level, allergies, and emotional factors.

The treatment for mild nausea is quite simple. Most women find that frequent, small snacks of dry foods, such as graham crackers, liquids in small amounts, and starchy foods are helpful. A simple trick that seems to work is to keep a couple of dry crackers at your bedside. Upon awakening, eat the crackers. This way, even if you do vomit, you will have something in your stomach bile. Your doctor may also prescribe some medication if necessary.

9. *Rhinitis*—Many pregnant women develop a post-nasal drip or a feeling of nasal stuffiness caused by a swelling of the mucous membranes of the nose and throat. This condition is called "pregnancy rhinitis." If the drip is annoying to you, it can be treated by using nose drops or a vaporizer or by having your physician prescribe an appropriate medication.

10. *Increased salivation*—Normal pregnancy is often accompanied by an increase in secretion by the salivary glands. This is often associated with an increase in nausea and vomiting. There are drugs of various types to treat this condition, if required. In general, the symptom disappears after the third month.

11. *Dental caries*—The old theory that the mother's teeth decay and decalcify to provide calcium and phosphorus for the fetus is not valid. There is no direct evidence of the adverse effect of pregnancy on healthy teeth. However, chronic inflammation of gums is common in pregnancy and usually increases in severity as pregnancy progresses. This is due to the increase in estrogen hormones in pregnancy, which increase the blood supply and thickness of the gums. Routine dental care should be practiced during the course of pregnancy and the use of local anesthetics for the treatment of dental caries is perfectly all right.

Surgery during Pregnancy

The chances are great that an expectant mother will not have to face the problems of surgery during pregnancy. However, should the occasion arise, it is reassuring to know that when a condition requires surgery, the appropriate operation can be performed, and the patient and fetus are usually not harmed. In fact, delaying surgery in such conditions as appendicitis is probably worse for the pregnancy.

The most common causes for requiring surgery during pregnancy are appendicitis, diseased gall bladder, trauma to limbs such as broken bones, ovarian cyst operations, suspicious breast masses, dental surgery of an emergency nature, and suspicious cancerous lesions. Your doctors will distinguish between emergency surgery which must be done here and now and elective surgery which is up to the patient and can be left until after delivery.

My own advice to pregnant mothers is to postpone any elective surgery. Each patient is an individual with an individual physical and emotional need, and the best course is to follow your own physician's advice.

Anesthetic techniques have now been sufficiently developed so that if surgery is required, safe precautions can be undertaken. Oxygen will be administered along with the anesthetic to the mother so that both mother and fetus will have plenty to go around. Even such specialized and dramatic operations as open heart surgery can be safely performed during pregnancy when necessary. Another common obstetrical indication for surgery during pregnancy is the treatment of the incompetent cervix syndrome discussed in another chapter. A large experience with this type of surgery during the first and second trimesters of pregnancy has shown that both the fetus and mother can tolerate anesthetics of various types without difficulty if required.

5
DIET AND NUTRITION
IN PREGNANCY AND LACTATION

METABOLISM AND NUTRITION
IN PREGNANCY

All our lives, we eat to satisfy hunger or to maintain good health, but once the food enters our mouths, we seldom think more about it except occasionally to see the results of what we eat in the form of excess body fat. But pregnancy gives new meaning to eating. By watching the baby grow, we can literally see food nutrients change into body tissue. And while this seems like a direct cause-and-effect relationship—increased food intake equals fetal growth—the mechanism does not really work that way.

Pregnancy is a time of change of all systems in the body. As mentioned in Chapter 2, metabolism is altered to allow the foods we normally eat to provide more than the average amount of nutrients to the body. Yet some changes in and additions to regular diet are suggested for the period of gestation. The only sources of nutrients for the developing fetus are the daily food intake and the body's store of nutrients. During the nine-month gestation, very rapid growth and development occur. The fetus is a parasite on the mother, but the old belief that the developing baby takes whatever it needs from the mother, regardless of her nutritional status, is no longer accepted. Research has shown that if the mother is not well nourished, the baby may be partially affected. Many studies have shown that the general nutritional state of the mother prior to and during pregnancy is important to the health of her baby. Studies during World War II on the effect of starvation on pregnancy confirm this fact. Some complications of pregnancy such as anemia, toxemia, and premature birth may result from an inadequate diet.

I cite all of these facts mostly as background since the greatest nutritional problem of middle- and upper-class Americans is excessive intake. As Jean Meyer, the Harvard nutritionist, says, "Americans produce the most expensive urine of any people in the world." Urine is the waste product of human metabolism. Other nutritionists show that Americans eat more sugars and starches than protein, calcium, fats, or all other nutrients put together. For pregnancy, then, you will probably not need to increase the amount of food you eat. You may, however, have to change the nature and amounts of the compounds in your diet.

To be well nourished during pregnancy, you should rely heavily on proteins, minerals, and vitamins in your diet. These nutrients are extremely important to support the growth of fetal tissue, and they are more important to your health than increased calories. A slice of cheese, for example, is rich in protein and calcium and contains fewer calories than a doughnut or a brownie. This makes it a far more preferable choice for a snack.

Actually, good maternal nutrition begins before a woman even becomes pregnant. Those who start off underweight are more likely to deliver small babies, even if they eat and gain normally during pregnancy. Women who are obese when they conceive are more likely to have difficulties with delivery and to develop high blood pressure.

Pregnancy, however, is not the time to shed extra weight. Dieting during pregnancy can deprive the fetus of adequate nutritional support. Also, the breakdown of fat that occurs with excessive dieting can release toxic substances called ketone bodies that could harm the pregnancy.

BASIC PRINCIPLES OF NUTRITION IN PREGNANCY

Weight Gain

Two generations of American physicians have taught their patients to impose dietary restrictions in pregnancy with the view of limiting weight gain to between 16 and 18 pounds. It is now known that on the average, 24 to 26 pounds is the appropriate amount of weight gain consistent with the most favorable outcome of pregnancy. Individual weight gain should be kept reasonably close to this average. However, thin or undernourished women should be encouraged to gain more than this. The rate of gain is also important. A pound and a half to three pounds the first three months, and 1 pound every nine days thereafter is average. The few pounds of fat the mother stores are needed for nursing. Most of the weight gain occurs in the last three months because that is when the fetus is growing at the greatest rate. Women who start pregnancy at a normal weight do best if they gain about 24 pounds and those who start out underweight should gain 30 pounds. A weight gain of more than 32 pounds is not recommended no matter how thin the mother was when she conceived. Ideally, weight gain in pregnancy should be gradual, though early nausea and vomiting may lower the increase in the first trimester. While severe weight restrictions may prove harmful to mother and baby, excessive gain may result in permanent obesity with its resulting complications of heart disease, high blood pressure, and diabetes. Some of it may not appear until late in life. Many women who gain excessive weight during pregnancy will lose it after delivery. Too many women who do not immediately return to their normal weight retain the excess and must diet to get rid of it. Nutrition in pregnancy, therefore, is a delicate balance of taking in the right nutrients without overdoing or dieting. Explaining this balance really makes it sound more complicated than it is to maintain it. Even women with minimal will power will find the motivation to do right by their babies more than adequate to ensure proper nutrition without making a big deal about dieting.

Calories

During pregnancy, you will need to consume an extra 300 calories a day, assuming you maintain your normal level of activity. This is the caloric cost of pregnancy. That's only the amount in a generous scoop of ice cream, so you obviously can't eat everything in sight. Rather, you have to make those added calories count toward the extra nutrients you need, and in pregnancy, there is an increased need for protein, calcium, iron, and the B vitamins.

Calcium

Milk or milk equivalents, like cheese, yogurt, or cottage cheese, are the best source of calcium. Milk doesn't have to be drunk; it can be added in liquid or powder form to soups, baked goods, cereals, and other prepared foods. Other calcium sources include broccoli, spinach, kale, and mustard greens, but the calcium from vegetables is less readily absorbed.

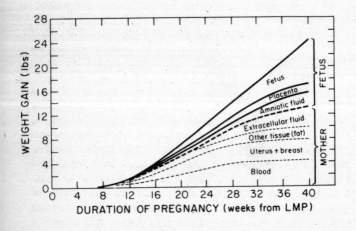

This figure depicts the weight gain in pregnancy. Most of the weight occurs after 20 weeks and is due to the many fetal and maternal factors as shown.

Four cups of milk or yogurt supply the daily recommended amount of calcium. The calcium equivalent of one cup of milk is supplied by one and one-half ounces of cheddar, one and three-quarter cups of ice cream, or two cups of cottage cheese. At the same time, a quart of milk would provide the needed amounts of vitamins A and D, two-fifths of the day's protein needs. If you can't drink regular milk because of inability to digest milk sugar, i.e., lactose intolerance, you should have no trouble with hard, unprocessed cheeses, like cheddar or Swiss, and you may be able to handle cultured milk products like yogurt and buttermilk.

Protein

In addition to milk to get enough protein, you would need to eat at least three servings of meat, fish, poultry, beans, peanut butter, or eggs a day. If vegetable protein is used to meet the day's requirements, be sure it's properly balanced in essential amino acids. This is achieved by combining grains with beans or nuts or by combining any of these dairy products in the same meal.

Iron, Vitamins, and Fluids

Good sources of iron include dry fruits, liver, kidneys, prune juice, and dried beans. However, few pregnant women consume enough iron; therefore, iron supplementation is recommended during pregnancy. Folic acid may also be given as a supplement since pregnancy doubles your folic acid requirement. It is found primarily in leafy green vegetables and in broccoli, asparagus, peanuts, and liver. Vitamin B_6 may also be needed in large amounts and it is found in whole grain bread and cereal, liver, spinach, green beans, bananas, poultry, fish, meats, nuts, potatoes, and green leafy vegetables. Liquids, some 6 to 8 glasses a day in addition to milk, are also important to maintain the increased body fluids of pregnancy and to counter the natural tendency to become constipated. Water, unsweetened fruit juices, and vegetable juices are your best sources of liquids. Excessive caffeine in some of the soft drinks are not recommended. Your doctor will probably supplement your diet with a prenatal compound which should prevent deficiencies of most vitamins and minerals. If your local water supply is not fluoridated, choose a vitamin with fluoride added.

Salt or sodium is no longer considered the cause of toxemia of pregnancy. Therefore, it is not necessary to restrict salt, which is actually increased in need during pregnancy. Remember the dangers of alcohol as outlined in previous chapters; don't drink more than an average of one drink a day on a regular basis. The amount of alcohol that is safe is still not known.

Some particular women who are pregnant need special attention to their nutritional needs. *Adolescents* up to 17 years old are still growing, and the stresses of pregnancy are added to the nutrient needs for body growth and maturation. Because they are growing, most girls under the age of 17 have greater nutritional requirements than adult women in order to keep their body size. When growth is completed, usually at age 17, their nutritional requirements during pregnancy are similar to those of mature women. Their increased nutritional needs should be worked out by their physician.

Other groups of women requiring special nutritional needs are *women from economically disadvantaged areas,* especially among minority groups. These women may have a low prepregnancy weight, and this is further magnified if it is followed by inadequate weight gain during pregnancy. Women who have frequent pregnancies, as often as a year apart, are also at greater risk for nutritional deprivation. Food faddists and constant dieters are at risk, and women with chronic illnesses, alcoholism, and malabsorption syndromes, may also be at risk because of their particular deficiency.

MENU SUGGESTIONS

As a general guide, remember: everything you eat or drink, except water, has calories. For the period of pregnancy, your goal is to find foods with maximum food value per calorie. This does not mean that all carbohydrates should be removed from the diet. A small or moderate amount of starches is needed to satisfy appetite and thus avoid overeating. The byword, though, is moderation.

Sample Meal Plan

This plan may help you. It contains a sample diet for one day based on a nucleus of protein-rich foods. These meals will be good for the whole family and can be altered easily to meet special dietary needs. Table I on page 52 summarizes the basic daily needs during pregnancy.

Breakfast:
    Citrus fruit—4 oz.
    Cereal (½ oz.) and/or bread and butter.
    Egg—1.
    Milk—8 oz.

Lunch:
    Protein dish such as nuts or cheese.
    Bread—2 slices as in a sandwich.
    Vegetables or salad.
    Milk—8 oz.
    Fruit—1 cup.

Dinner:
    Meat or equivalent—4 oz.
    Potato—1.
    Vegetable (½ oz. peas, ½ oz. string beans).
    Butter.
    Milk.
    Fruit or dessert.

Between Meals:
    Milk and/or fruit.

Iron-Rich Diet for Anemia

Anemia, a deficiency of red blood cells, usually results from an inadequate intake of iron in foods or faulty absorption of iron in the stomach. If anemia, as determined by the hemoglobin count, is diagnosed, a dietary supplement may be called for since healthy blood is so vital to overall good health. Many obstetricians believe it is important to provide the mother with iron therapy to prevent iron-deficiency anemia. Others maintain that an adequate protein diet is all that is necessary to acquire the additional iron needs and that deficiencies can be corrected by eating more liver and rare meats. In cases of very severe anemia, diet may be no help at all, and injections of iron may be required.

Nutrition in Lactation

If you plan to nurse, you should know that a woman's nutritional needs are even greater during lactation than in pregnancy. A nursing mother has to produce about a quart of milk a day to satisfy her baby. To do this, she will probably need an extra 1,000 calories a day above her prepregnancy diet. These calories should include an extra 40 grams of protein, at least a quart of milk a day, and additional eggs, cheese, butter, liver, and vegetables. Fluid intake should total two quarts to maintain the volume of milk produced.

TABLE I
BASIC DAILY PREGNANCY DIET

Predominant Nutrient	Foods	Number of Servings*
Protein and iron	Lean meats, fish, poultry, lentils, dried beans and peas, eggs, nuts	3 or more (7 oz.)
Protein and calcium	All milks, cheese, cottage cheese	4 or more
Vitamin C	Citrus fruits and juices, broccoli, brussel sprouts, greens, peppers	1 or more
Vitamin A	Fortified margarine, kidney, dark green and deep yellow vegetables	1 or more
Energy and B vitamins	Whole grain or enriched breads and cereals	5
Other vitamins and minerals	All fruits and vegetables	2 or more
Energy	Fats and sugars	Only as needed for energy

*A 2–3-oz. serving of lean cooked meat, fish, or poultry without bones is:

    ¼ lb. hamburger after it is cooked
    ½ cup cooked diced lean meat, fish, or poultry
    One medium meat or fish patty
    One slice roast meat or poultry, 5 × 2¼ × ¼ in.
    Two frankfurters
    Two slices of liver
    Two slices meat loaf
    Two medium chicken drumsticks (fryer)
    One chicken leg, including thigh
    One medium-sized fish steak

A substitute for a 2–3-oz. serving of lean cooked meat, fish, or poultry without bone is:

    ½ cup cottage cheese
    3 ounces cheddar or jack cheese
    1 cup cooked dried peas, beans, or lentils
    ½ cup shelled peanuts
    4 tablespoons peanut butter
    3 eggs

A serving of vegetable or fruit is:

½ to ¾ cup or a portion as ordinarily served such as:

    1 medium apple
    1 medium banana
    1 medium orange
    1 medium potato
    ½ medium grapefruit
    ½ medium cantaloupe

A serving of whole grain or enriched breads and cereals is:

    1 slice enriched or whole grain bread
    ½ to ¾ cup cooked whole grain cereal such as cracked wheat, oatmeal, brown rice, rolled wheat
    ½ to ¾ cup cooked enriched cereal such as grits, cornmeal
    ½ to ¾ cup enriched noodles, macaroni, spaghetti
    ¾ cup enriched ready-to-eat cereal
    ½ to ¾ cup rice, enriched or converted
    1 large enriched flour tortilla
    2 small corn tortillas

(Cross, A. T., and Walsh, N. E.: Prenatal diet counselling. *J. Reprod Med* 7:273, 1971)

6
PERINATOLOGY (THE FETAL WORLD)

Perinatology is the study of human development from a microscopic cell to the fully formed infant, floating gracefully in the liquid prenatal environment awaiting birth. As a science, perinatology has been of interest to biologists for many years. But only within the past two decades has it become a useful tool for the practicing obstetrician.

In 1963, Dr. A. William Liley performed the first recorded intrauterine blood transfusion, which marked the beginning of modern perinatology. The New Zealand physician, faced with a fetus severely weakened by Rh disease but too premature to survive early delivery, passed a needle through the mother's abdominal wall, through the uterus into the baby's abdomen, giving the fetus new blood and new strength to live. While this procedure might sound very matter-of-fact in today's chronicle of medical miracles, Dr. Liley's transfusion represented the first intrusion into the womb to help a developing fetus. Since then, doctors have come from this relatively simple procedure to opening the uterus during pregnancy, performing surgery on the fetus, and replacing the developing baby to continue gestation.

These are special uses of the science of perinatology, reserved for the few problem pregnancies. But the knowledge gained from this special work has contributed an invaluable amount of information about normal growth and development of the fetus. That is why a lengthy discussion of this subject is included in this book. It is my hope that the information given in this chapter will help you, as a mother-to-be, marvel at the intricacies as well as the beauty of birth and that this understanding will make the experience much less mysterious.

FETAL GROWTH AND DEVELOPMENT

Throughout most of pregnancy, the fetus is a completely formed, miniature human being who is active and quite lively. The unborn baby has senses of touch and hearing. It responds to pain, pressure, and loud noises. It sucks and swallows.

By the third month of gestation, the unborn baby has developed all the systems needed to maintain life after birth. The baby then spends the next six months letting those systems mature and get used to working together under the direction of the baby's master conductor, the brain. Toward the end of pregnancy, the baby develops a layer of fatty tissue just under the skin for warmth. This pattern of growth is truly amazing, but it is also quite deceiving. While the third-trimester growth is most obvious, the fetus actually grows at a much faster rate in the early months. During the first month of pregnancy, fetal weight increases 10,000 times. In the second month, it increases another 74 times. In the third month, growth increases only 11 times. In the last few months of pregnancy, the rate of growth falls to 0.3. But even if this rate of increase were maintained after birth, your child would weigh about 160 pounds by his or her first birthday.

Table I shows the average height and weight of the fetus at the end of the various lunar months of pregnancy. In general, the length of the fetus is a more accurate measure of its age than is its weight. The average birth weight of American babies is about seven pounds. Boys tend to be about three ounces heavier than girls at birth. Besides the baby's sex, birth weights are influenced by the socioeconomic status of the mother—which often determines her nutrition—the race and size of the parents, the number of children previously born to the mother, and a number of other factors. So that while seven pounds is the average, a normal, healthy full-term baby may weigh anywhere from 5.5 to 11 pounds at

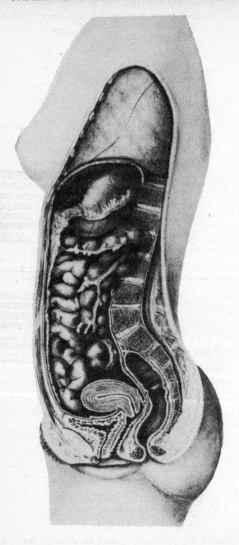

Cross section of mother before pregnancy showing small uterus.
Courtesy Maternity Center Association, New York City.

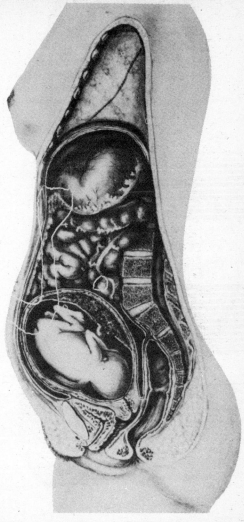

Five-month fetus lying within the amniotic cavity, showing the relationship of the placenta, umbilical cord, and fetus. The uterus is now at the level of the navel. *Courtesy Maternity Center Association, New York City.*

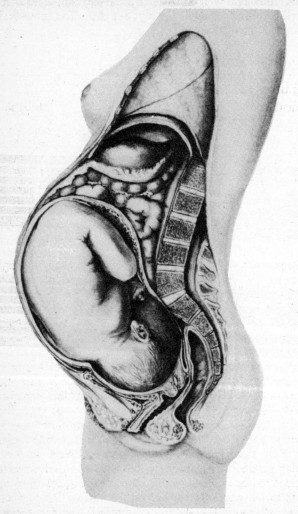

Nine-month fetus. The uterus occupies almost the entire abdominal cavity. The mother's lower stomach and intestines are crowded together and the diaphragm is pushed upwards. *Courtesy Maternity Center Association, New York City.*

birth, although weights over ten pounds are considered excessive. The infant weighing less than five pounds is considered premature.

TABLE I

Lunar Months	Weeks	Weight	Height
3	9	½ oz.	3.5 ins.
4	16	4 ozs.	6.2 ins.
5	20	11 ozs.	8.8 ins.
6	24	1.3 lbs.	11.7 ins.
7	28	2.2 lbs.	13.7 ins.
8	32	3.7 lbs.	15.6 ins.
9	36	5.5 lbs.	17.5 ins.
10	40	7.0 lbs.	19.5 ins.

Along with physical growth, the developing baby is sharpening its five senses, which will help him sort out his environment and negotiate his way in the world. If the unborn baby were not confined to the darkness of the womb, it would probably be able to see and distinguish gradations of light. Doctors suspect this from observing the behavior of premature infants, who have this ability at birth.

More fascinating is the development of the fetus's sense of hearing. While in the uterus, the fetus is bombarded with many different sounds: its mother's heartbeat, the grumbling of her digestive tract, the echo of her voice. Some specialists believe that loud outside noises penetrate the closed uterine environment of thin women. An interesting experiment grew out of the suspicion that the fetus hears and reacts to sound during gestation. A nursery for the newborn in one hospital decided to play a recording of a slow, steady heartbeat in one room to see what effect it had on the babies. The newborn infants who were exposed to the amplified heartbeat seemed to be calmer and better eaters than the infants in an adjacent nursery, in which the heartbeat was not played. Many young mothers are applying the results of the experiment themselves by placing a soft-ticking clock in the cradle or crib of their newborn infants.

Fetal movement occurs very early in pregnancy, but is not usually perceived by the mother until after the fourteenth week. This early perception is called "quickening" and can be influenced by such factors as the amount of fat the mother has in her abdomen. While most of the early movement is reflex action, later movement may be caused by discomfort or pressure. During prenatal examinations, when the doctor measures fetal growth by feeling the abdomen, the baby inside often changes position. A more dramatic illustration of fetal sense of touch can be seen during a diagnostic procedure called "amniocentesis." Amniocentesis, an analysis of the amniotic fluid, requires the insertion of a small needle into the uterus through the abdominal wall. Sometimes, the fetus is struck inadvertently and responds with violent kicking, amply demonstrating its displeasure.

THE PLACENTA AND UMBILICAL CORD

The placenta is a perfectly marvelous organ. This smooth, glassy barrier serves two main functions for the fetus, which depends on it for its existence. First of all, the placenta produces the hormones to keep the body primed for pregnancy. Then it serves as a kind of Berlin Wall—selectively letting substances come and go from mother to baby, and vice versa. It transfers respiratory and nutritive materials to the fetus and collects the wastes of respiration and metabolism, all the while keeping two separate circulatory systems between mother and baby.

The placenta enhances the passage of gamma globulin from mother to baby. Gamma globulin, a blood protein, contains the antibodies against disease, so that the baby receives his mother's immunity.

The placenta also acts as a physical barrier between the mother and the fetus. In other words, the fetus is actually a transplanted foreign element within the mother which she will tolerate for nine months before expelling it. In fact, some people hypothesize that labor is initiated by the mother's body rejecting this "foreign transplant."

In addition to its very basic functions, the placenta changes throughout pregnancy to adjust to the size and needs of the baby. For instance, as the baby gets bigger and needs more food, the cells of the placenta thin out, allowing nutritive material to pass through more easily. This thinning phenomenon is called the "increasing permeability" of the placenta.

The placenta seems to possess certain selective powers that allow it readily to pass calcium, gamma globulin, and proteins—all important to fetal growth—into the fetus at concentrations higher than those in the mother. The placenta also passes easily most substances composed of small molecules. From a practical standpoint, you should be aware that almost all drugs are made up of small molecules and pass readily from mother into fetal blood and tissues. It is also believed that some bacteria and viruses pass through the placenta, resulting in an occasional infection of the fetus. Rubella or German measles virus can result in fetal malformation if it is contracted during the first trimester of pregnancy.

FETAL CIRCULATION AND RESPIRATION

Fetal circulation differs from circulation after birth for several reasons. First of all, very little fetal blood passes through the lungs. Instead, blood is purified of carbon dioxide and filled with oxygen and nutritive material in the placenta and is carried to the fetus through the umbilical vessels.

The lungs are collapsed until a few seconds after birth, when blood is forced in with the baby's first breath. Special ducts which were used by the fetus to bypass this pulmonary circulation are simultaneously closed. There is a small opening from the right side of the heart to the left side called the "foramen ovale." This also closes once circulation in the lungs has been established. If the foramen ovale remains opened, circulation disturbances can result which may require treatment after delivery.

THE FETAL HEAD

All of fetal development can be considered a marvelous engineering feat. But the best-designed feature in the overall body structure is the fetal head. The head is composed of bony portions, not firmly united but separated from one another by spaces filled with membranes called "sutures." The design allows the head, the largest single part of the baby, to compress, change shape, and adapt to the contours of the birth canal during labor. The compressibility is called "molding" and will be discussed in more detail in the next chapter.

The two most important spaces are the frontal suture and the sagittal suture in the base of the skull. The frontal suture is covered with a membrane called the "fontanel," which is more commonly known as the "soft spot" on top of the baby's head. After birth, as the baby gets older, the sutures fuse, giving the child the closed skull of the adult.

As labor approaches, the head of the fetus usually settles into the narrow opening of the uterus, with legs, feet, thighs, and buttocks filling out the wider portion of the pear-shaped organ. Ninety-six percent of all babies conform to uterine contour this way, using the shape of the womb in the most efficient manner for labor.

AMNIOTIC FLUID

Throughout pregnancy, the fetus floats in a fluid medium called "amniotic fluid." This fluid serves several purposes. It helps the developing baby maintain body temperature. It serves as a shock absorber against injury. It allows the fetus easy motility. It is also known that the fetus continually drinks the fluid. Since amniotic fluid contains protein and carbohydrates, it also may provide some nutrition for the fetus.

The actual source of amniotic fluid is not completely clear, but very early in pregnancy, it begins to collect in the space left between the wall of the placenta and the fetus itself. This space is called the "amniotic cavity." The amount of fluid may be as little as a cup at three months' gestation and as much as a quart at term. The composition of the amniotic fluid changes throughout pregnancy, and it reflects the sum total at any one time of fetal swallowing, fetal urination, fetal circulation, and size.

Because the amniotic fluid also contains cells shed by the fetus, an analysis of the fluid can also give us much information about the health and well-being of the growing baby. For example, the sex of the fetus can be determined by an analysis of cells within the fluid. Other tests tell fetal age. Still other tests allow doctors to detect many genetic abnormalities early in pregnancy.

WAYS TO EVALUATE FETAL HEALTH

During the past two decades, knowledge of the intimate world of the human fetus has greatly accumulated. This information helps us improve the quality of human birth. In fact, the fetus has rightfully achieved the status of the second patient.

A variety of techniques have been developed and are of value in appraising the health of the fetus. These include amniocentesis, amnioscopy, fetoscopy, ultrasound, measurement of certain hormones and chemicals in the mother's blood, special fetal heart rate tests, and actual measurement of the fetal blood during labor for toxic products. These new procedures have certainly contributed to the improvement in fetal health that has occurred. However, other factors have also contributed to this accomplishment. There are certainly less unplanned and unwanted pregnancies since the legalization of elective abortion. Pregnant women are taking greater advantage of pregnancy care. There has been an increase in the availability of excellent neonatal care, and greater attention has been paid to the fetus with the techniques of monitoring fetal well-being during labor. In addition, there has been an increased use of Cesarean sections to try to minimize fetal risks of various types.

Knowledge of these procedures will help you understand how the second patient, your fetus, can be checked and cared for.

AMNIOCENTESIS

The analysis of the fetal fluid that allows us to find out all these things about the fetus is called amniocentesis. Amniocentesis has become a major tool of the perinatologist—and for good reason. It is highly accurate. Though it generally is safe and simple in the hands of an expert, there is some potential risk. It represents one of the major advances in obstetrical practice of the past decade.

Amniocentesis is performed by passing a long needle through the abdomen and the uterine wall into the amniotic cavity under ultrasound guidance where a small portion of the fluid is removed. It has become useful in the management of many complications of pregnancy including diabetes, toxemia, hypertension, Rh disease, postmaturity, and repeat Cesarean sections. This diagnostic tool is used in the following cases:

1. *Rh disease*—Rh disease occurs in pregnancies in which the mother's blood type is Rh negative and the husband's is Rh positive. The designation positive or negative is derived from a substance present in most humans' blood and the bloodstreams of all rhesus monkeys. To have the substance is to be Rh positive and not to have it means one is an Rh negative. Rh disease can occur because many women at delivery received a small amount

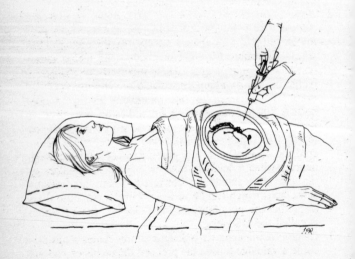

The technique of amniocentesis is illustrated in this figure.

of the baby's red blood cells in their own bloodstream following delivery of the placenta. Usually this slight mixing causes no problem, but in those pregnancies in which the mother is Rh negative and the father is Rh positive and the baby inherits a positive factor, something strange occurs. The mother reacts to this foreign blood by producing antibodies which stay in her blood system. Then if the next baby is also Rh positive, these antibodies cross the placenta and cause slow destruction of the fetus's red blood cells. With progressive destruction of red cells, the fetus can become severely anemic. The degree of fetal anemia can be determined by analyzing the amniotic fluid, especially for its bilirubin contents. Bilirubin is a breakdown product of red blood cell destruction. By analyzing the amniotic fluid for bilirubin, the doctor can tell the degree of anemia the fetus is experiencing and can, on that basis, decide on treatment. Rh disease has been markedly diminished today by the development of antibodies given as a preventative much like a vaccine (see Rh Disease, Chapter 11).

2. *Respiratory distress syndrome or hyaline membrane disease*—This disease is a lung condition of many premature infants who can die of respiratory failure. This disease is caused by a peculiar substance which forms on the surface of lung tissue, blocking the exchange of oxygen and carbon dioxide across the membranes of the lung. The cause of hyaline membrane disease is not known but appears only in infants who are alive at birth. A new test on amniotic fluid has been developed to tell which babies may develop this disease if delivered too soon. This test is utilized in complicated pregnancies when a decision is to be made as to whether or not the fetus should be delivered. There are various substances which can be measured in the amniotic fluid to predict the possibility of lung disease, one of which is called the L/S ratio.

3. *Genetic amniocentesis*—Genetic amniocentesis has become a valuable tool in the prenatal diagnosis of various birth defects. Although this is a well-established procedure, it still generates some controversy, since the physician is generally unable to treat the disease that

is being diagnosed, leaving termination of pregnancy as the usual alternative. (See Chapter 12 for more on genetics.)

Indications for Genetic Amniocentesis

A. *History of chromosome abnormalities*—Chromosomes are tiny structures present in every human cell. Each chromosome contains thousands of genes that are critical to an individual's growth and development and that determine hereditary traits. Each normal human cell, except the egg and sperm cells, has 46 chromosomes. They can be photographed and arranged into 23 matching pairs as illustrated. In the normal reproductive cycle, the mother's egg containing 23 chromosomes is fertilized by the father's sperm, also containing 23 chromosomes. This union results in the development and growth of the fetus, whose cells have the normal number of chromosomes, 46. Serious birth defects usually result if there are too many or too few chromosomes. The most common chromosomal abnormality in newborns is an extra chromosome in the 21st pair. This results in a disorder called "Down's syndrome," formerly called mongolism. It has been known for a long time that the risk of having a baby with Down's syndrome increases with the mother's age, especially after 35. Recently, it has been shown that the extra chromosome can come from the mother or the father. When either parent has had a child with a chromosomal abnormality of some type, there are at least one or two chances in 100 that a subsequent child will have severe birth defects associated with chromosomal abnormalities. For some specific types of chromosome abnormalities, the risk is even higher. The chromosomes of the fetus can be studied from the fetal cells in amniotic fluid. The fetal cells are grown in tissue culture. After 3 or 4 weeks, they can be analyzed for these chromosome abnormalities.

B. *Maternal age*—The most common indication for genetic amniocentesis today is maternal age. Most experts recommend that amniocentesis be performed starting at age 35, as the risk of having a live-born infant with Down's syndrome at age 35 is 1 in 300; at age 40, it rises to 1 in 100; and in 45-year-old-mothers, the risk is 1 in 30. However, increased maternal age predisposes to other chromosome abnormalities,

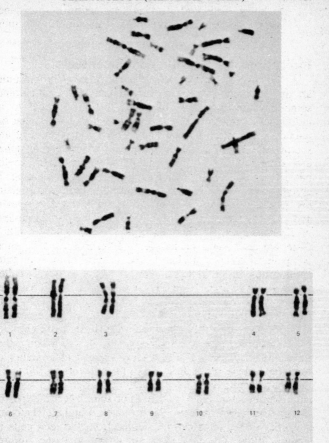

Figure shows chromosomes after arrangement into pairs showing 23 pairs. The XX pair predicts a female.

too, so that the risk of any chromosome abnormality between ages 35 and 39 is 1 in 70.

C. *Previous Down's syndrome*—If a couple has had a previous child with this syndrome, the risk of recurrence is at least one percent regardless of age.

D. *Carriers of sex-linked disease*—There are some genetic disorders, such as hemophilia, which are manifested by virtue of the sex of the offspring. For instance, in hemophilia, 50 percent of the male offspring will have the disease and 50 percent will be normal. Daughters will be either carriers or normal, but none will have the overt disease. Parents at risk face the difficult decision of pregnancy termination involving all male fetuses with the discomforting knowledge that half of them would be completely normal.

E. *Carriers of autosomal recessive diseases*—Amniocentesis is also indicated when both parents are known to be carriers of so-called autosomal recessive diseases. These diseases include Tay-Sachs disease, Neiman-Pick disease, Hurler's syndrome, galactocemia. Perhaps over 60 to 70 of these can be now diagnosed *in utero*. In all such cases, there is a 25 percent chance that the offspring will have the disease.

F. *Neural tube defects*—Neural tube defects are defects caused by poor development of the spinal canal or skull overlying the brain. This can give rise to defects called anencephaly, spina bifida, or meningomyelocele. If one parent was born with a neural tube defect or has had a prior child with this abnormality, the incidence of a similar problem in subsequent offspring is 3 to 5 percent. This figure rises as high as 10 percent if the family already has two children with this type of problem. The presence of this defect can be clued in by measuring a substance called alpha-fetal protein in the amniotic fluid, and confirmation of the defect can be carried out by ultrasound measurements and evaluation.

Complications of Amniocentesis

Amniocentesis is relatively safe; however, certain risks must be considered as in any medical procedure. The risk of complications from amniocentesis should be weighed against the chances of having a child with special problems. Mild complications for the mother may include cramping, bleeding, and leakage of amniotic fluid. Fortunately, these problems occur only 2 or 3 times in 100 cases and usually require no treatment. For those few women with Rh negative blood, additional medication may be needed after the procedure to prevent Rh sensitization.

Serious complications from amniocentesis, such as miscarriage and injury to the infant, develop infrequently, probably in the order of 1 in 200. One of the most severe theoretical complications of amniocentesis is miscarriage. A miscarriage can occur during any pregnancy, usually during the early weeks. However, even after the third month of pregnancy, 3 or 4 out of every 100 pregnancies end in miscarriage. A large study in the United States, however, showed that amniocentesis did not significantly increase the chance of having a miscarriage. The possibility of the needle's pricking the fetus is always present, but fortunately, serious effects from this are very uncommon.

Remember, however, that birth defects which do not represent chromosomal abnormalities, such as cleft lip and palate, congenital heart disease, and club feet, are not picked up by this test. A normal result from prenatal chromosome and AFP testing will not guarantee a normal baby. A decision about amniocentesis for prenatal testing has medical, financial, emotional, and ethical implications to the entire family. You must weigh the risks and benefits of having amniocentesis in light of your chances of having a baby with an abnormality and how that would affect your family.

Fetal Age Determination

Fetal age can be fairly accurately determined by the amount of a substance called creatinine found in the amniotic fluid. Creatinine is secreted in the fetal urine into the amniotic fluid. After 37 weeks of gestation, the amount of creatinine in the urine and therefore in the amniotic fluid rises sharply. By analyzing this substance, a doctor can tell if the fetus is relatively mature; however, the L/S ratio for lung maturity is a more useful test.

Fetal Sex Determination

As outlined above, fetal sex is determined as a byproduct of chromosome analysis. A male has an XY pair and a female has an XX pair. This accurate method comes after centuries of trying to figure out ways to determine the baby's sex before birth. Supernatural and other methods have been developed, going back to Egyptian and Chinese cultures. Any other method of determining the sex of the fetus is really useless other than chromosome analysis, including such commonly cited methods as fetal heart rate, fetal position, size of the abdomen, and fetal activity, despite what your grandmother says.

ULTRASOUND

Imagine a technique that can look inside a two-month pregnancy and see the beating heart of the tiny fetus or see, at three months, the separate sacs of a twin pregnancy or, at any stage of pregnancy, continuously measure the growth of the fetus. All this safe and without harm to the mother or fetus. This is the new technique of sonography.

Sonography is probably the single most successful method of intrauterine diagnosis that has evolved in recent years. It has greatly enhanced our diagnostic abilities in pregnancy for evaluating the health of the fetus. The sonographic methods available now, carefully performed and accurately interpreted, supply vital information about the health and status of the fetus with no known risks.

Ultrasound uses sound waves of high frequency (above the normal range of hearing) sent out by a scanner. The waves reflect back from the object to be studied, giving a "picture" of that object. Ultrasound was first used in industry to detect flaws in construction metal, and later, as sonar to locate submarines below the surface of the water. When ultrasound is used in medical equipment, the wave frequency is very high, but the power of the sound wave is extremely low.

Sound is a physical force in no way related to x-ray. The sound wave is produced by a small crystal called a transducer placed on the surface of the body. The sound waves, or vibrations, enter the body and echoes are reflected when they strike the surface of a body organ—a baby within the uterus, fluid, bone, etc. The echoes are converted into electrical signals and transferred to a screen, where internal organs and the structures are outlined in detail and their characteristics seen. These pictures on the screen may be photographed, and a physician with special training studies them to gain valuable information.

The sonographic technique can be used in a number of ways: (1) It can measure the size of a structure, such as the fetal head; (2) it can give you a cross-sectional picture which can allow us to identify the size, shape, and locations of the structures, such as the fetus or the placenta; (3) it can be used to observe actual movements of structures (this is called real-time sonography), as in a beating fetal heart. In real-time sonography, a special transducer is used which produces multiple echoes which are tripped off in sequence and therefore detect movement. Fetal movements, fetal cardiac motions, and vessel pulsations can be seen.

There are mainly two forms of ultrasound now used in pregnancy. One is the real-time ultrasound for visualizing movements, and the other technique is called the B-scan which gives a cross-sectional picture of greater detail than the real-time sonography.

Ultrasound has many specific uses in obstetrics, some of which are as follows:

1. The early identification of an intrauterine pregnancy—A fetal sac can be seen within the uterus as early as three and one-half to four weeks after conception.
2. Demonstration of life of the fetus (the beating heart) can be seen as early as six weeks from conception or eight weeks from the last menstrual period.
3. Twins or other multiple births can be identified quite early, probably with accuracy by the second or third month.
4. By measuring the width of the fetal head, the so-called biparietal diameter, we can identify the stage or duration of pregnancy. When measured serially, the biparietal diameter can determine whether the fetus is growing normally and give an estimate of "due date."
5. A comparison of normal fetal head measurements, chest and abdominal measurements can pick up early major abnormalities in this area.
6. Other major fetal abnormalities of the kidneys, intestines, and limbs can also be determined.

7. Problems with the amniotic fluid, either too much (hydramnios) or too little (oligohydramnios) can be picked up.

8. The placenta can be localized both for problems, such as placenta previa (see Chapter 11) or for visualization purposes during the technique of amniocentesis.

9. Rare placental abnormalities, such as molar pregnancies, can be determined.

10. Any extra tumor masses or developmental abnormalities of the uterus can be identified. An example of a uterine tumor is a fibroid. In addition, ovarian cysts present during pregnancy can be followed by serial measurements.

11. Intrauterine devices, so-called IUDs, can be seen on sonography if necessary.

12. The biophysical profile of the fetus, including breathing movements and tone, can be seen.

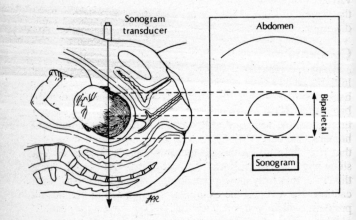

The method for measurement of the fetus's biparietal head diameter is illustrated in this figure.

Preparation for the Examination

To enable the doctor to read the pattern of echoes from the pelvic structures and a baby inside the uterus, it may be necessary for you to have a full bladder during the examination. You may be a little uncomfortable from your full bladder for a short time, but you should not experience any other discomfort. No injections, special medications or special diets are required before the examination.

Ultrasound is usually performed by a ultrasound technologist or a physician. You will lie on your back on an examining table or bed, and your abdomen will be uncovered from the lower part of your ribs to your hips. Mineral oil will be placed on your abdomen so the tip of the ultrasound instrument, called a transducer, can be moved easily across your abdomen. The oil coating also improves penetration of sound waves into your body. You will not experience any discomfort during the examination except for a small amount of pressure from the instrument as it is moved across the abdomen. The hand-held tip of the instrument is placed on the abdomen and moved to various positions. Photographs are taken of the pictures on the screen so the doctor may look at them later and make a diagnosis. The examination usually takes 30 minutes or less.

Concerns

Many people today express concern about the possible long-range effects of ultrasound and damage to the mother or baby. No damage has been reported to the mother or unborn baby after using ultrasound for 15 years in medical centers throughout the world. Studies have been done on animals and humans, including babies, and there is no evidence to date that it is harmful. Although extensive use and tests do not show any danger associated with diagnostic ultrasound, since this is a relatively new procedure, it should be used with caution. However, if the examination is needed to diagnose a problem which you or your baby may have, the benefit obtained from this information far outweighs the possible slight risk that might be involved.

Cost

The cost of your examination varies from one institution to another and with the length of time required to do the examination. It usually costs about the same as an x-ray examination done for the same purpose. Check with your health insurance representative to determine if an ultrasound examination is covered, in whole or in part, by your policy.

FETOSCOPY

Recently, a small group of doctors have been trying to develop an instrument for directly looking at the fetus and the placenta. The advantage of this instrument would be to pick up early abnormalities as well as to allow the direct procurement of red blood cells from the fetus by taking blood directly from the fetus or placenta. Abnormalities, such as sickle cell disease, can be diagnosed early. Fetoscopy is still regarded as a research procedure because of its risk and limitations. Perhaps by the third edition of this book, techniques will be worked out that actually peer safely into the previous inviolate world of the fetus.

HORMONE AND ENZYME MEASUREMENTS

During pregnancy, a variety of chemical substances called hormones or enzymes are produced by the fetus, placenta, mother, or various combinations thereof. These various substances have been extensively studied with the hope of discovering practical means of measuring fetal health and age. The names of some of these substances are placental lactogen, estriol, chorionic gonadotropin, and progesterone. Your physician may use some of these tests, especially in pregnancies complicated by postmaturity, high blood pressure, diabetes, etc. Repeated measurements of these substances may aid in monitoring the health of the fetus.

FETAL MONITORING

Accurate ways to keep track of the fetal heart rate are now available. This technique is called fetal monitoring. Fetal monitoring can be used prior to labor, as in the so-called antepartum nonstress test. During labor, electronic monitoring can be used to watch and record the fetal heart rate and contractions of the uterus.

Both techniques utilize two major aspects. One is a method for picking up the fetal heart. This can be done by ultrasound, electrocardiogram, or sound itself, either by pick-ups on the maternal abdomen or electrodes directly attached to the fetal head during labor. The other aspect is a method for monitoring the duration and strength of the uterine contractions. This can be done by a pressure device on the mother's abdomen or a pressure device in the uterus itself.

When fetal monitoring is done prior to pregnancy, the nonstress test is used. This technique depends on the physiologic fact that the fetal heart rate increases when the fetus moves. The presence of this fetal heart rate increase indicates a healthy baby. The absence of the fetal heart rate acceleration associated with fetal movement casts a suspicion on fetal well-being. If a nonstress test suggests that the fetus is in some difficulty, other more definitive and complicated tests are performed to further evaluate the situation. The nonstress test has become a routine screening device for monitoring fetal well-being prior to labor in cases where there is a suspected problem.

During labor, in many institutions, fetal monitoring has become almost routine. When a woman is in active labor, transducers are placed on her abdomen, one to follow uterine contractions and the other to monitor fetal heart rate. The field has evolved so that very sophisticated patterns of alterations of fetal heart rate in association with uterine contractions can fairly accurately predict when the fetus may be in jeopardy. There is no question that fetal monitoring has saved the lives of many infants that previously were not suspected of having difficulties *in utero*. Most centers use fetal monitoring as a screening device as well as for determining the strength, frequency, and duration of uterine contractions.

If the fetal monitoring suggests a problem in fetal well-being, an additional test called fetal scalp blood sampling can be performed during labor if the cervix is partially dilated. This technique uses a device for obtaining a minute quantity of blood from the fetus's scalp which can be measured quickly for evidence of fetal distress. The blood is measured for the amount of acid-base balance, the so-called pH test. If this technique shows fetal distress by a fall in the pH, immediate delivery is indicated, often by Cesarean section.

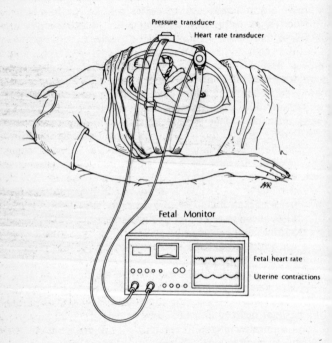

The technique of fetal monitoring is illustrated in this figure. Separate recordings are made of the fetal heart rate and uterine contractions from separate transducers.

Most obstetrical services have shown that with the increased use of electronic fetal monitoring, there has been an appreciable increase in the Cesarean section rate. Whether these two are directly related is not clear. Recently, a medical task force concerned with the various facets of the difficult problem of predicting fetal distress during labor has reached certain conclusions. Their conclusions about monitoring the fetus electronically during labor have been summarized as follows in the sixteenth edition of *Williams Obstetrics* (Appleton-Century-Crofts: 1980):

Methods introduced into obstetrics in the last decade may conflict with the concept of family-centered childbirth. Electronic fetal monitoring, however, need not diminish the human experience of childbirth if properly employed and explained by supportive people. Pregnant women who have the opportunity to discuss potential usage and limitations of monitoring are less likely to have a negative reaction to its use. The routine use of electronic fetal monitoring should not necessarily increase the Cesarean delivery rate. The use of fetal scalp blood sampling provides additional help in reducing the incidence of monitoring-associated Cesarean sections. The routine use of monitoring in low risk pregnancies is not necessarily beneficial, but its use when risk factors increase seems to be beneficial.

Clinical Monitoring

The state of the fetus can also be satisfactorily monitored by well-trained individuals during labor without electronics. The fetal heart rate is measured at frequent intervals during and right after uterine contractions until delivery. Heart rate between contractions will average about 140 beats per minute but should be no less than 120 and no more than 160. Fetal heart rate should not change appreciably during or after uterine contractions. Clinical monitoring also is valuable in producing healthy outcomes.

7
LABOR AND DELIVERY

LABOR

While standing at the stove one Friday evening, preparing a hefty, completely indigestible roast beef dinner, Mrs. Barbara Nichols sensed a "funny feeling" in her abdomen. "Could it be the beginning of labor?" she asked herself. Her baby was "due" in two days. After working into her ninth month of pregnancy, she had just completed household preparations the day before: the house had been cleaned thoroughly, the baby's furniture had been delivered and assembled. And, since she was an impatient person generally, she was ready for delivery.

But was this really labor? The feeling was not a pain. It more resembled a mild charley horse—a muscle tightening, increasing in intensity and subsiding. If this were truly labor, the "feelings" would have to become progressively stronger, occurring more frequently. They did.

After dinner, Mr. Nichols asked about the evening plans: "Are we going to the movies or not?"

"We can," she replied, "but I think you should know I have been having these feelings for the last two hours. They have come regularly—every 15 minutes. I think they are contractions, but I am not certain."

"Well, when were you going to tell me?" her husband asked in mock outrage. "Are we going to the movies?"

"Yes," she replied.

So, taking the bag along, they drove to the movies and relaxed for two hours. Mrs. Nichols remembered that her childbirth class had told her that first babies do not fall out—and she was in no hurry to go to the hospital.

When the movie was over, the contractions were coming about every four minutes. Mr. Nichols called the doctor from the theater, and he suggested they go to the hospital. Five hours later, the baby, a eight-and-a-quarter-pound boy, was born.

Mrs. Nichols' approach to this process known as labor was a very relaxed one, for good reason. While labor is one of the most dramatic points in the pregnancy, it is really just a period of adaption. There is a baby at one end of the birth canal, and the body is trying to expel it. The physical process which allows this to happen is called "labor." The three important factors in this passage are the *expulsion power of the uterus, the passage through which the fetus must pass, and the fetus itself.*

Components of Labor

1. *The fetus*—The position of the fetus in the uterus is a crucial factor in the course of labor, because it determines the adapting process. Most babies—96 percent to be exact—settle head down in the uterus and are born that way. The head-first birth is called a "vertex presentation." In a small percentage of all deliveries, the feet or backside of the baby presents itself first. These positions are called "breech presentation." Since the moment of birth is marked by the delivery of the shoulders, breech babies are the only ones whose sex can be determined before they are actually "born." Even more rarely, a baby will settle across the abdomen, rather than up and down, which requires operative delivery if the fetus cannot be coaxed into a vertical position.

   There is variation in fetal position even in the vertex presentation. Three-quarters of all babies born head first come out of the birth canal facing the mother's back. The remainder face the front of her body. In this latter position, called a "posterior" position, the baby's bony skull is in contact with the mother's spine; she may feel labor pains in her back rather than in the abdomen.

The prevalence of the vertex or head-first presentation is not totally understood by doctors. As mentioned in the last chapter, one theory suggests that the fetus tries to utilize uterine space most economically, choosing the position which best fits the shape of the uterus. Another theory says that the force of gravity is responsible for the head assuming the downward position. The two theories do not necessarily cancel each other out.

Another indication of the natural tendency for babies to be born head first is the construction of the head itself. The fact that it is made up of small bones joined by membranes, rather than one mass of bone, would tend to support this assumption. The construction of the head makes it somewhat compressible so that it can adapt to the shape of the birth canal. This process is called "molding." Molding can affect the appearance of the fetus at birth. It is quite common for firstborn infants to have marked molding.

2. *The pelvis passage*—The diameter of the pelvis passage must be wide enough to accommodate the birth of the baby. Most pelvises are. Occasionally, however, a woman has an unusually narrow pelvis or may have suffered some change in contour in an accident, in which case the baby is delivered by a Cesarean section. Measurement of the pelvis can be taken by internal examination. More accurate measurement can be made by a special x-ray called "pelvimetry," usually performed if the baby's head has not dropped into the pelvis passage prior to labor.

3. *The expulsion process*—The baby is pushed out of the mother by two forces: the involuntary contractions of the uterus, and the involuntary and voluntary contractions of the mother to push the baby out.

True labor begins when the individual muscles of the uterus begin to contract together, acting like one big muscle. In early labor, contractions can be very irregular, occurring every 15 or 20 minutes. The interval between the contractions gradually decreases so that toward the end of labor, they are occurring every two or three

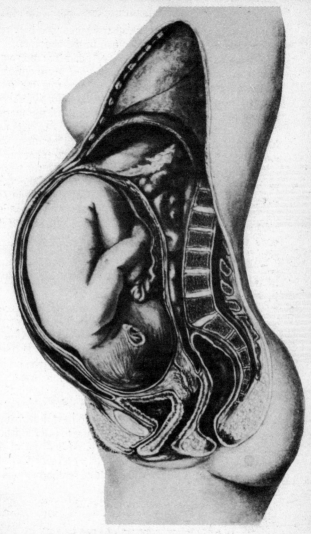

Term-size fetus with the head engaged within the pelvic cavity prior to onset of labor. *Courtesy Maternity Center Association, New York City.*

minutes. Each contraction lasts from 30 to 90 seconds—early contractions are usually shorter; later contractions longer. Certain breathing exercises aid the contractions by supplying more oxygen to the abdominal muscles. This, in effect, relieves tension in the muscles, lessening the feeling of tightening of the contraction (see Chapter 8).

In addition to these factors, birth is enhanced by the pressure of the descending baby on the pelvic floor and rectum. The pressure causes a bearing-down reflex which is similar to that involved in defecation. The reflex can be controlled to some extent by conscious attempts of the mother to push the baby out.

The uterus and cervix play a role here, too. As term is approached, the lower part of the uterus begins to get thinner. The cervix, the door to the uterus, loses its long thick character—it gets shorter and thinner in a process called "effacement."

The Stages of Labor

While most women think of labor as one continuous process, labor really has three distinct stages, each with its own landmarks and characteristics. The first stage begins with the first contraction and ends when the cervix is fully dilated. The second stage picks up at full dilation and ends with the delivery of the baby. The third stage consists of the delivery of the placenta.

1. *First stage*—During pregnancy, the cervix undergoes continuous change in preparation for labor. It gets progressively softer and spongier. It also gets shorter and the cells thinner in order to facilitate dilatation. This shortening and thinning of the cervix is called "effacement." Before effacement, the cervix is about an inch and a half long. After effacement, it has virtually disappeared.

   Once the cervix becomes this thin, the contraction force of the uterus and the pressure from the baby's head gradually force the opening wider, until it is big enough to permit the baby's head to pass through. This is similar to trying to put your head through a turtle-neck sweater, but slowly. This process is called dilatation.

Full dilatation is set at ten centimeters, about the width of a hand. Women who have had babies before may be slightly dilated (two centimeters) before the onset of labor.

2. *Second stage*—There are several forces at work to aid the passage of the baby through the birth canal. Uterine contractions, which helped dilate the cervix, are now even stronger, forcing the baby down and out. The contractions, which were coming about 15 minutes apart in the beginning, are now occurring every 2 to 3 minutes, lasting 60 to 90 seconds each. As the baby descends, the mother begins an involuntary bearing down, more commonly known as "pushing." The head descends and is delivered slowly, followed by a rapid expulsion of the rest of the baby's body.

3. *Third stage*—After the baby is delivered, the uterus sheds the placenta, which nurtured the fetus during its nine months' gestation. The uterus continues to contract even after the birth of the baby. It begins to get smaller, and its wall thicker, reducing the surface to which the placenta was attached. The placenta tears away finally and is pushed down and out of the vagina. Blood clots immediately begin to form at the site of separation, preventing any excessive bleeding. Bleeding after delivery of the placenta is also controlled by the uterus contraction down and closing the blood vessels that had previously supported the placenta.

What Happens in Labor and Delivery

One or two weeks before you actually begin labor, you may notice intermittent contractions of the uterus. The contractions will feel like a tightening of an abdominal muscle or a dull ache or pressure in the lower pelvis or lower back. You may feel the baby drop down into the pelvis at this time. This settling-in is called "engagement," because the baby has fixed itself in position for birth. From the mother's perspective this same phenomenon is called "lightening" because the baby's new position is giving her a little more space to breathe and digest food.

During this period, the mucous plug of the cervix, which protected the baby from vaginal germs, may dislodge. You

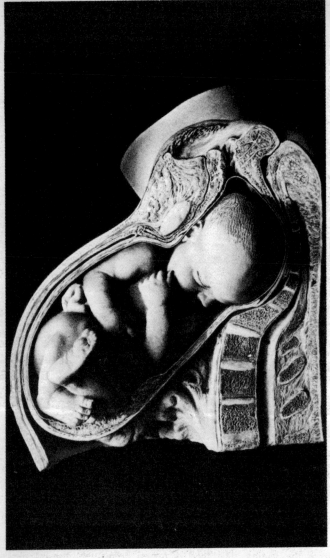

Full dilatation of the cervix with membranes intact at the onset of the second stage of labor. Delivery of the fetal head. *Courtesy Maternity Center Association, New York City.*

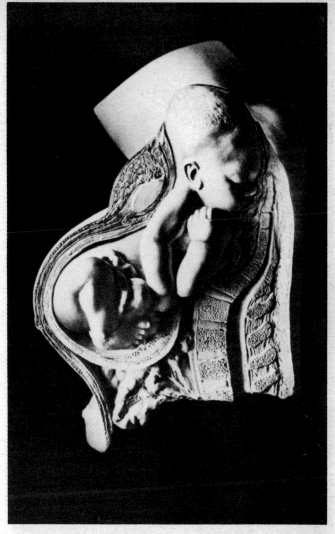

Crowning of fetus's head beginning actual expulsion of the fetus from the vagina. The face is turned completely toward the mother's back. The mother's perineum is stretched around the fetus's head. *Courtesy Maternity Center Association, New York City.*

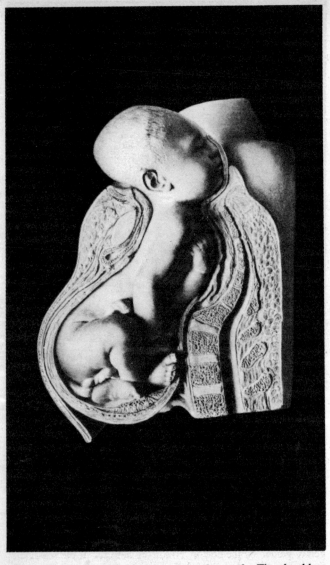

Baby's head continues to emerge as head extends. The shoulders are also turning. *Courtesy Maternity Center Association, New York City.*

Head completely delivered. Notice head returning to transverse position so that shoulders can then be delivered. The head is gently guided by the doctor. Following delivery of the shoulders, the rest of the baby's body slides out. At this point baby might even cry or breathe spontaneously. *Courtesy Maternity Center Association, New York City.*

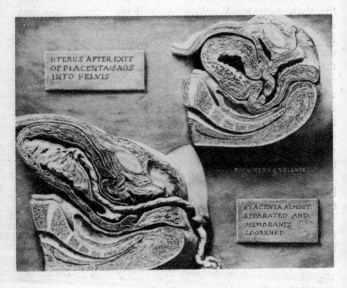

Third stage of delivery. The placenta tears away and is pushed down and out of the vagina by the mother with the aid of the doctor. *Courtesy Maternity Center Association, New York City.*

will be able to tell this has happened because vaginal discharge will be thicker and pink or a little deeper red. The membranes of the amniotic sac may also rupture as the baby settles down. While the rupture of membranes most often occurs rather late in labor, in about 20 percent of all women, the membranes break before labor. If this occurs, you may expect as much as two pints of clear, watery liquid to leak from your vagina. If this does happen, you should call your doctor, who may advise you to go to the hospital. A tear in the amniotic sac means that the baby is more susceptible to infection. There will be no question in your mind as to whether or not your membranes have broken. There is no discharge that can be confused with this time. In any case, either of these two events—the dislodging of the mucous plug or the rupture of the membranes—is a welcome sign to mothers, who can be pretty certain that labor will start relatively soon.

But the question most mothers-to-be have is: How do you know when you are in labor? The answer to that question is that you might not know at first.

It is often very difficult to distinguish the intermittent contractions that occur before the beginning of true labor from the contractions of real labor. As a rule of thumb, remember that true labor pains are regular and persistent. They gradually increase in frequency and duration and get stronger.

So-called false labor, known as "prodromal labor contractions," are irregular and tend to disappear if you lie down or walk around. They do not increase in frequency or duration.

Early in the first stage of labor, when the cervix is starting to dilate, contractions are most often felt in the back. You will be aware of them, but they will not interfere with normal activities. If it has not happened already, the mucous plug will dislodge.

As labor progresses and the contractions increase in frequency and length, the cervix slowly dilates. The rate of dilatation varies, being slower in women having their first babies than in women having second or third or fourth babies.

For new mothers-to-be, it will take an average of eight and a half hours for the cervix to dilate two and a half centimeters,

Clinical Course
of Primiparous Labor

1st stage of labor is divided into latent phase of approximately 8 to 9 hours and active phase of cervical dilatation (2 to 4 hours) followed by 2nd stage of labor.

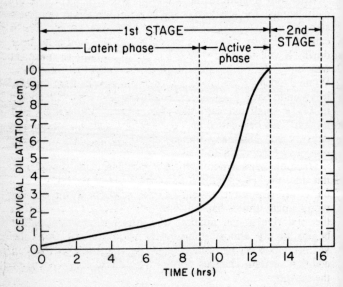

Figure depicts the stages of labor and cervical dilation. The first stage is divided into latent and active phases. Note that the latent phase, when little dilatation occurs, occupies most of the first stage. The active phase is when most women will enter the birthing facility.

one-fourth the amount of dilatation necessary for birth. Do not panic about the length of time. It most often goes unnoticed, which is why it is called the "latent phase" of the first stage of labor. You probably will not even know you are in true labor until the latent phase is completed.

The latent phase is followed by an accelerated or active phase, during which time the cervix dilates from three to ten centimeters (full dilatation). This phase takes an average of 2 to 4 hours. This is the phase of greater discomfort and usually you will be in a labor room by now.

The average length of the total first stage of labor for a woman having her first baby is about 12 hours. For women who have had a baby before, full dilatation takes about seven hours.

After full dilatation, the second stage of labor automatically begins. The pressure of the baby on the pelvic floor will start the involuntary pushing reflexes described earlier. These can be aided by the voluntary efforts of the mother to bear down. It will take a first baby close to an hour to make its way down the birth canal, through the vagina to the vulva. When the baby's head can be seen at the mouth of the vagina, it is said to have "crowned." Following crowning, the doctor makes a small cut into the area between the vagina and rectum. This cut, called an "episiotomy," allows for quicker delivery and eliminates the possibility of the baby's tearing muscles of the vagina or vulva.

Once the head is delivered, the baby turns one shoulder to the side, then eases out the other. The rest of the body slides out easily. Upon the entrance of the newborn to the outside world, many things happen, and many changes occur within the first five to ten minutes of birth. The newborn infant begins to cry almost immediately upon its exit from the vagina. Upon crying, active breathing is established, and in addition, certain changes occur in the circulatory system of the newborn.

The cause of an infant's crying, taking its first breath, has been speculated upon for many years. It still remains something of an enigma. Various explanations have been suggested. They include physical stimulation, that is, the handling of the infant due to delivery's provoking and stimulating the infant, or the accumulation of carbon dioxide due to oxygen deprivation. Whatever the cause of the first cry, it certainly is a welcome sound to those present in the delivery room.

The mother may receive medication to facilitate delivery of the placenta. After that happens, the episiotomy is sewn up, and the mother can relax.

Going to the Hospital

Once you determine that you really are in labor, you should call your doctor about going to the hospital. You will probably be consciously aware of contractions for about two hours before you call him. If contractions are coming every 15 minutes—for an hour—it will still take some time to confirm the criteria for labor—regular, progressive, stronger. It is wise during this time to limit food intake to Jell-O or liquids. Solid foods or an excessive amount of fluid may cause vomiting during labor, which could be hazardous if anesthesia is being used.

When contractions are coming about every five minutes, your doctor will probably tell you to go to the hospital. Exactly where in the hospital you report should be worked out with the admitting office beforehand, if possible. After admission, you will be sent to the labor floor, put in a separate labor room and examined internally by a nurse or a resident physician, who will be able to tell the amount of cervical dilatation and the position of the fetus. This professional will listen to the baby's heart by placing a stethoscope on the abdomen or by placing you on the fetal monitoring unit. The normal fetal heart rate varies between 120 and 160 beats per minute. A rate less than 100 may indicate some problems. This is why fetal heartbeat is listened to so often during labor.

Following this initial examination, which is reported in full to your doctor, an enema is given to remove all fecal material from the rectum. While women generally shudder at enemas, most women in labor welcome them. By removing a source of pressure in the pelvic area, the enema makes labor more comfortable.

As a sanitary measure, the pubic hair may also be shaved from the vulva. Some hospitals are eliminating this measure as standard procedure because the whole perineal area is doused with antiseptic before birth anyway. An alternative procedure, called a "mini-prep" is just the removal of the small amount of hair at the episiotomy site and serves the purpose just as well.

During labor, your doctor will examine you vaginally several times to check the progress of dilatation and the position of the baby. Doctors perform only a necessary number of these examinations to minimize the possibility of infection.

When you are fully dilated, you will be taken to the delivery room for the actual birth, then to a recovery area where bleeding and post-delivery contractions are checked, before being taken to your room. You may remain for up to two hours in the recovery area, during which time the nurse may press on your abdomen frequently to check on uterine tone, before being taken to your room. Many hospitals have instituted special labor and delivery suites called "birthing rooms." These all-inclusive rooms have special labor beds that can be turned into delivery setups so that you do not have to be moved. These birthing rooms also tend to be less antiseptic in nature and some have even the amenities of TV and telephone. You can call your family yourself with the news, "boy or girl."

Management of Labor

There are basically two ways of making labor more comfortable. The doctor has a number of analgesics or anesthetics that are perfectly safe to use during labor. Or a mother, with the help of her husband, can practice what is commonly called "natural childbirth." This term is a misnomer because it seems to imply a passive participation by the mother. Actually, natural birth in this country is psychoprophylactic childbirth, or the Lamaze method. This approach involves a number of breathing and body-building exercises, as well as a secondary conditioning to labor. This method is discussed in detail in Chapter 8.

These two ways of managing labor are not mutually exclusive. Many women who take pain-killers or anesthetics know and practice parts of the Lamaze approach. Likewise, Lamaze-trained mothers are not wed to a drug-free labor. Many have gone through the childbirth course to involve their husbands more actively in the birth process. They are not necessarily committed to the whole regimen.

Analgesics and anesthesia for labor and delivery—Today, a variety of drugs are used to relieve pain of a woman in labor. The need for such relief is, of course, highly individual and variable, depending upon a number of things, such as the woman's ability to withstand pain, the size of the baby, the size of the mother's pelvis and birth canal. There is no method that assures 100 percent relief from pain of labor, but modern chemical technology has made it possible to be a comfortable experience.

Scopolamine is one of the drugs that are useful in labor. It works by inhibiting secretions in the gastrointestinal tract and by depressing the central nervous system, reducing fear and excitement. It is relatively harmless to the baby. In the right dose, it also produces drowsiness and amnesia. It is most often used along with a pain-relieving drug. The most popular of these is a synthetic narcotic with the trade name of Demerol.

Demerol decreases pain, but it also depresses breathing. Since it is a drug that crosses the placenta, in high doses it may depress the breathing of the baby as well, which may require the use of respiratory equipment to help the baby breathe after birth. Premature babies are especially susceptible to the effects of Demerol. Doctors try to avoid using it in the few hours before delivery for just this reason. Correctly used, however, Demerol is a very valuable drug for pain relief in labor.

Barbiturates do not decrease pain. They are used in labor, however, because they help allay fears and may produce sleep. These drugs, too, should be avoided late in labor to prevent depression of the newborn.

Tranquilizers are also used during labor to calm the mother and decrease nausea and vomiting. They sometimes increase the effectiveness of the analgesics, such as Demerol, without an increase in dosage. They are well tolerated by the mother and have little, if any, effect on the newborn. They produce a state of relaxation that increases the mother's ability to participate in labor and delivery.

Besides analgesics—pain relievers—the obstetrical bag of tricks includes anesthesia—drugs that cause a loss of feeling, either all over the body or just in the area affected by birth. On April 7, 1853, John Snow administered chloroform to

Queen Victoria during the delivery of her eighth child, Prince Leopold, and initiated the use of anesthesia in obstetrics.

A variety of inhaled and injected substances are now used as general anesthesia for delivery. General anesthesia had been very popular over the past few decades, but recently has lost some favor. More and more women are wanting to see the birth of their baby, which is not possible with general anesthesia but is possible with regional anesthesia. Then there is the problem of vomiting under the influence of general anesthesia. If vomiting occurs while the mother is sleeping, the food she throws up may be breathed into the lungs, causing pneumonia.

The most common regional-anesthesia techniques today are the spinal, epidural, and caudal. In addition to allowing the mother to see the birth and avoiding the dangers from vomiting, regional-anesthesia techniques do not pass significant quantities of drugs into the fetus. They can, therefore, be used during labor as well as delivery.

There are some disadvantages with these techniques. They require an experienced, skillful doctor to administer them so that they are completely effective. They require the cooperation of the mother also. Occasionally, some mothers have toxic reactions to the regional drugs, which means a mother must be supervised very closely after they are administered.

1. *Spinal*—A spinal anesthesia involves injecting the chemical agent into the spinal canal, eliminating pain in the pelvic area and in the legs. Although it can be used for labor, it is generally used only for delivery. Spinal anesthesia carries with it an increased possibility of headaches in the week following the baby's birth and a possible drop in blood pressure during delivery, which can be treated.

2. *Epidural or caudal*—This type of anesthesia consists of injecting small doses of the anesthetic agent into the canal surrounding the spinal column. The outgoing and incoming spinal nerves pass through this canal and receive the effect of the drug at that time. When successfully administered, it removes the pain of labor within a few minutes without interfering with uterine contractions. It also seems to relax the pelvic muscles and hasten cervical dilatation, thereby shortening the first stage of

labor. But it also lessens the mother's ability to push the baby out, which means that this type of delivery is often aided by the use of forceps. Forceps delivery is not difficult, but the administration of the drug is. This is why the caudal or epidural anesthesia is not available at all hospitals. In expert hands, this method approaches the ideal method of pain relief in labor and delivery. It has a minimum of side effects, and can be administered during the first stage of labor, and it allows the mother to be awake for and participate in the birth of her child.

3. *Local*—There are also "local" anesthetics. A drug, usually novocaine, is injected into the area where the episiotomy is to be performed. This drug is very useful for uncomplicated, simple, spontaneous delivery. The drugs have no effect on the fetus and wear off very soon after delivery.

A different local anesthesia is the paracervical block, which involves injecting anesthetic drugs into the nerves entering the cervix during the first stage of labor. The agents are supposed to block sensation in these nerves, and the pain associated with cervical dilatation is therefore eliminated. The technique is only about 80 percent successful, however, and it is not easy to administer or comfortable to the mother.

While all of these methods of making labor more comfortable are available to most practicing physicians, each physician has his favorite. It would be wise for you to talk with your doctor about labor and delivery and the use of medication during each, to make certain that his preferences are the same as yours. If possible, you can map out a primary approach, flexible enough to change during labor if you decide it is necessary.

How to Deliver a Baby in an Emergency

The likelihood of you not delivering in the hospital is remote. However, virtually every physician has had at least one patient who was unexpectedly delivered outside the hospital with no doctor present. These patients are usually women who have had many children before and just can't make it to the hospital in time. Taxis, elevators, ambulances, and hospital lobbies are well-known sites for these events.

The best way to avoid an emergency childbirth is to recognize the physical signs that announce the delivery is coming. Often your physician will do weekly pelvic examinations in the last month. If a woman has fast or early labors, the presence of some cervical dilatation will warn you and him to the possibility of a quick labor. Certainly, with the history of fast, quick, painless, early labors, a heightened awareness of these factors will prevent these problems from arising. If a mother in labor leaves for the hospital when her contractions are coming every ten minutes or less, she should have no trouble getting there in time in the normal instance. However, rarely the occasion will arise when it is not safe to speed the mother to the hospital, and once the baby's head can be seen, preparations should be made for emergency delivery.

The qualifications required to deliver a baby under emergency conditions are common sense, calm attitude, and patience. Ambulance attendants and policemen are trained to be good emergency midwives. Clean, if not sterile, conditions are desirable. Clean linens or even clean newspapers will do. If possible, sterile scissors and clean or sterile shoelaces, cord, or string should be available. The person going to deliver the baby should wash his hands and arms thoroughly. Patience is not just a virtue in delivery, it is a necessity. No attempt should be made to hasten the delivery by pulling the baby or by yanking on the cord. Just let the baby come out naturally. As the head appears in the birth canal, the deliverer should stand to the left of the mother, place his left hand just below the infant's head, cradling it as it emerges but not interfering with this motion or attempting to turn it. If, as occasionally happens, the baby's umbilical cord is wrapped around its neck, the cord should be loosened, but it need not be untangled until after delivery. Once the baby's head is delivered, the rest of the body will follow naturally and quickly.

The baby's first breath often requires some assistance. If possible, the most efficient way to clear the infant's air passages is to aspirate its nose and mouth with an ear syringe. The traditional method of holding the baby up by the heels and smartly spanking its bottom is still effective. If at all possible, aspiration of the nasal and throat passages should be done as soon as the baby's head is delivered. Tying and cutting the umbilical cord takes place after the baby is fully emerged. No attempt to cut it should be made until the cord has become limp, pale, and pulseless. One shoelace, strip of cloth, or string is tied firmly around the cord halfway between the mother and the baby, and the other is tied about four inches away from the first. The cord is then cut halfway between the ties with sterile scissors.

Expulsion of the placenta after birth will usually come about 15 minutes after the cord has been cut. To help bring about this natural process, the baby may be placed on the mother's breast with its face to the nipple. The baby's sucking triggers a reflex reaction which causes the uterus to contract and push out the placenta. The delivery of the placenta is usually followed by some vaginal bleeding. However, this will slow down sooner if the mother lowers her legs and places them together and the uterus of the mother is massaged through the abdominal wall. The uterus can be felt just above the pubic bone as a large firm mass. Massaging will quickly produce a tightening of this mass and a decrease in the amount of vaginal bleeding.

The mother may be taken to the hospital as soon as the placenta has been expelled. Remember to take the placenta along so that it can be examined for its completeness. The vaginal area should be carefully cleaned with water and covered with a sanitary napkin. The mother and baby should be taken to the hospital in an ambulance if possible.

I hope this information is not necessarily used; however, remember, don't panic. Babies have been born thousands of years prior to the invention of midwives or obstetricians.

OTHER TYPES OF DELIVERY

Throughout this book, when I have referred to birth, I have meant vaginal birth. As mentioned earlier in this chapter, most babies are born through the vagina, head first. Not all babies come into the world this way, however, and not all vaginal births are the same.

Forceps Delivery

Many vaginal births are aided by forceps, metal instruments that resemble scissors or salad tongs. They can be used to remove the baby's head from the mother's pelvis without injury to baby or mother. They can also be used to help rotate the fetal head to put the baby in a better position for birth. Some anesthesias inhibit the expulsion process, necessitating the use of forceps in delivery.

If forceps delivery frightens you, it should not. The use of this instrument in obstetrics got a very bad reputation because doctors in the past used them to reach high into the birth canal, requiring a good deal of force to extract the baby. Today, however, forceps are not used unless the cervix is completely dilated and the head is within two inches of the mouth of the vagina. Indications for forceps delivery can be summarized as follows:

1. Elective forceps—to aid in completion of second stage.
2. Prolonged second stage—if a patient has been in second stage of labor for more than two hours, forceps delivery is indicated. This may be due to poor contractions, large fetus, and/or small pelvis.
3. Maternal emergency—such as shock or exertion.
4. Fetal emergency—slowing of fetal heart rate, indicating some fetal distress.

Forceps delivery, as practiced today, is very safe.

Cesarean Section

Cesarean section is the removal of the baby by making an incision in the abdominal wall, then in the uterus. The term comes from the *lex caesarea*, which required an abdominal postmortem delivery of any woman who died in childbirth. It has come to mean delivery of any child by abdominal operation.

Over the past ten years, certain factors have led to an increased Cesarean birth rate. Twenty years ago, obstetricians accepted a Cesarean rate of 3 to 5 percent as normal. Today, most obstetrical services are reporting Cesarean birth rates of 20 to 25 percent, which includes repeat Cesareans.

Cesarean deliveries were once feared. But the improvement in surgical techniques, in preoperative and postoperative care, and in reducing infection has made the use of Cesarean section a safe procedure for the indicated patient.

We have become increasingly aware that Cesarean birth

results in a healthier infant than prolonged labor and difficult vaginal delivery. Advances in monitoring the baby during labor have permitted earlier detection of infants who will not tolerate vaginal delivery.

A C-section is a major surgical procedure which may unexpectedly have to be performed. It should not, however, be viewed as failure on the part of either the mother or the obstetrician. The ultimate goal is a healthy mother and child.

The most common reasons for Cesarean delivery are the following:

1. The mother's pelvis is too small to allow passage of the baby.
2. The baby is positioned abnormally, such as across the abdominal cavity, rather than vertical to it.
3. The uterus is not contracting with enough force to push the baby down.
4. Previous Cesarean.
5. Pelvic tumors.
6. Fetal distress.
7. Abnormalities of the placenta such as placenta previa or placenta abruptio.
8. Maternal diabetes and pre-eclampsia.
9. Rh disease.

In the first edition of this book, I wrote that a previous Cesarean section was an indication for a repeat operation in a subsequent pregnancy. However, many recent reports have shown that women can be safely delivered vaginally after a previous Cesarean section if the following criteria or safeguards are followed:

1. The previous Cesarean section was a so-called low segment type of operation, i.e., the incision was in the lower part of the uterus. If a classic Cesarean section has been performed—that is the incision was made in the top of the uterus—it is absolutely necessary to deliver all subsequent babies by Cesarean prior to labor.
2. The previous indication for the first Cesarean section is no longer present, such as would be the case in fetal distress or placenta previa or breech delivery, and, of course, no new reason is present.

3. The trial of labor for vaginal delivery is closely monitored and facilities for emergency care, such as blood transfusions and surgery, are closely present.
4. The pregnancy involves a single fetus in the vertex (head first) position of less than 8.8 pounds.

If these criteria are followed, some hospitals have delivered normally as many as 80 percent of these patients with previous Cesarean sections. The risks of uterine rupture in these cases is less than 1 percent, and the rupture is usually not catastrophic for mother or baby.

The classic dictum, "Once a Caesarean, always a Caesarean," no longer appears to be true.

Preparation for Cesarean Delivery

Before the operation is performed, a nurse will prepare you. Certain medications may be given to help dry secretions in your mouth and upper airway, and the lower part of your abdomen will be washed and may be shaved to remove any hair. A catheter is placed in the bladder before surgery to keep the urinary bladder empty. This decreases the risk of injury to the bladder during the operation and aids delivery of the infant. An intravenous will be started permitting fluids to be given during the operation. Certain medications that might be required are also given through the IV.

If there is time and no emergency is present, the anesthesiologist will discuss the various types of anesthesia available and may allow you to indicate your preference. Anesthesia for Cesarean section may be either regional or general. Regional anesthesia consists of either spinal or epidural anesthesia. This allows you to be awake but numb from just above the waist to your toes. If general anesthesia is chosen, you will be asleep throughout the operative procedure. Either method is safe in the hands of a competent anesthesiologist.

In many hospitals, the patient's partner may accompany the mother to the operating room and be present during the Cesarean birth. If the father is to be present at a Cesarean birth, he will be expected, before entering the operating room, to change into appropriate clothing provided by the hospital.

The Operation Itself

The surgeon makes an incision during the Cesarean birth through the wall of the abdomen. It may be either vertical or midline incision from the navel to the pubic bone or may extend from side-to-side just above the pubic hairline, a so-called "bikini" incision. The choice of skin incisions is at the discretion of the surgeon performing the Cesarean birth. After the abdomen has been opened, an incision is made in the wall of the uterus in order to deliver the baby. This incision, too, may be either vertical or transverse. The transverse incision is used more frequently since it is made in the lower part of the uterus. The vertical incision, however, is sometimes needed for certain positions of the baby and certain other medical emergency situations. After the baby is delivered through these incisions, the placenta immediately follows. Following delivery of the baby and placenta, the incisions in the uterus and abdomen are closed with sutures.

After the surgery, you usually will be taken to the recovery room. During this time, your blood pressure, pulse rate, and respiration rate will be checked regularly, and you will be observed for excessive vaginal bleeding. If regional anesthesia was given, you will see your baby at delivery and will probably be allowed to hold him or her for a while before the infant is taken to the nursery for observation. Early contact between parents and baby following Cesarean birth is beneficial to both and allows early bonding. That is one reason why I prefer regional anesthesia for my Cesarean deliveries.

Postoperative Care

You will usually be kept in bed for the first day of delivery. During this time, you will be encouraged to move about. After the first day, you will be advised to get out of bed with help by a nurse or other responsible persons. The bladder catheter is removed soon after surgery, and you should be able to resume voiding without difficulty. IV fluids are continued until you are able to take fluids and nourishment orally. IV fluids are usually required only for the first 24 to 48 hours.

For several days after the operation, the abdominal incision will be uncomfortable. You may request, however, medication for relief of pain as on order by your physician. Your duration of hospital stay following a Cesarean birth depends on the rapidity with which you are able to resume your normal functions. In most instances, discharge from the hospital following a Cesarean can be anticipated within seven days. The stitches or clips in the abdominal incision will usually be removed between days five and seven after surgery.

Complications and Risks

Cesarean section in the past 20 years has become an increasingly safe operation to perform. The advances in anesthesia technique, blood banks, surgical care, and antibiotics have reduced the risks to the mother. Improvements in the care of the newborn infant have also occurred, making this safer and more suitable for the baby. There are, however, risks involved which any mother should be aware of. Complications that may occur are infection, blood clots, excessive blood loss, and occasional complications from anesthesia. However, treatment is available, and these complications are usually temporary.

Following a Cesarean delivery, you will rapidly regain normal body function and after 4 to 6 weeks should be able to resume full activity without real limitations. Breast-feeding should not be limited by Cesarean delivery. Because of the increasing percentage of Cesarean births, many centers have set up special antepartum classes, programs, and support groups for couples anticipating Cesarean delivery. Cost of Cesarean birth is more than vaginal delivery because of the increased length of hospital stay, the necessity for anesthesia, and the cost of using an operating room and its personnel and equipment. In the last analysis, your physician can best answer your questions and concerns regarding Cesarean section.

Induction of Labor

Sometimes, doctors have to induce labor artificially. Most often, it is done for certain medical reasons. These reasons might include toxemia, diabetes, Rh disease, postmaturity, and high blood pressure. Labor is induced generally by injecting into the mother a hormone called "Pitocin," which brings on uterine contractions and labor. This same hormone is used for women who are in labor but whose contractions are not strong enough to dilate the cervix or push the baby down.

Pitocin increases the intensity and frequency of contractions. It is quite powerful, and its use must be supervised at all times. Pitocin is very valuable in the management of labor when used correctly.

There are a number of theoretical benefits of elective inducements. The mother is well rested prior to labor and is psychologically prepared for it. Her stomach will be empty of food, limiting the risk of vomiting after having anesthesia. There is no last-minute rush to the hospital, causing problems of where to put the children. The risk of delivery at home or rapid labor is avoided. Delivery can be set during the day, when hospitals are better staffed. In short, elective induction of labor can ensure peace of mind, constant medical attention, and orderly hospital admittance, and it allows the mother enough time to organize her family responsibilities.

But not every woman is a candidate. She must be very near term. The fetal head should be engaged and the general size of the baby adequate. In addition, the cervix must be soft and ready for induction.

However, the elective induction of labor is still a very controversial procedure. Some obstetricians feel that any interference with the natural process of labor and delivery should be avoided. Perhaps the family and the medical profession should accept a little inconvenience for so special an event. Of course, the ultimate question of induction of labor rests in your discussions with your physician, since he is the best person to evaluate the suitability, availability, and possibility of its use. During the past ten years the elective induction of labor seems to have become less popular.

ALTERNATIVE BIRTHING PROCEDURES

Birthing Room

Many hospitals in the U.S. offer the option of having your baby in a birthing room. In it, a woman can go through labor, delivery, and recovery without the physical strain of changing rooms. Birthing rooms are decorated with all the comforts of home—paintings on the wall, drapes, comfortable chairs, TV, phones—and your husband and maybe even your children will be allowed to be there for support.

The advantage is that it eliminates some of the psychic stress of a hospital environment and is more like having a baby in your own home. However, the room is still in a hospital with all the proper backup medical equipment and talent nearby in case of emergency.

Childbearing Maternity Centers

An alternative to having a baby in the traditional hospital maternity section is the childbearing maternity center. These facilities are run by trained nurse-midwives usually close to a maternity hospital. To cut the risks of childbirth, such centers carefully screen and monitor patients during the antepartum period to ensure that no high-risk pregnancies or difficult deliveries will be encountered. Adequate screening and good transport facilities are basic to these programs.

One of the primary attractions of these centers is that generally costs are less than in a hospital.

Their use and safety are still being evaluated by the medical community.

8
PSYCHOPROPHYLAXIS— THE LAMAZE METHOD

The psychoprophylactic method of prepared childbirth (PPM
originated in the Soviet Union and was based largely on the
work of J. P. Pavlov on the theories of the conditioned
response. In 1950, the method, which was already being used
extensively in Russia, was presented by Dr. A. P. Nicolaiev
of Leningrad to the World Congress of Gynecologists which
was held in Paris and which was attended by a French
physician, Dr. Fernand Lamaze. That presentation greatly
interested Dr. Lamaze, and the next year, while visiting
Russia, he studied the method and witnessed its successful
use by Russian women in labor. He was so impressed with
what he saw and heard that on his return to France, he began
his dedicated efforts to introduce the method there, making
only some slight modifications which he felt were suitable for
Western culture.

The popularity of the method spread rapidly in France; it
was well established in China and the Communist countries
and, following sanction by Pope Pius XII in 1956, began to
be used in the more Catholic-oriented countries of southern
Europe and South America.

Thus, in less than a decade, PPM (which refers to the
psychoprophylactic method) was being used in many countries
almost circling the globe, with the remarkable exception of
the United States. A brief attempt to introduce PPM in

Cleveland, Ohio, was made by a Swiss physician, Dr. Isador Bornstein, but because of illness, his work had to be abandoned prematurely. In 1958, Dr. Bornstein's book *Psychoprophylactic Preparation for Painless Childbirth* was published and is believed to be the first book on the method written by a physician in the United States.

Shortly after this, however, came the first real introduction of the method in the United States, in New York, largely due to the efforts of an American mother and writer, Marjorie Karmel, who had used the method with the birth of her first baby while living in Paris. The first experience had been so satisfying to Mrs. Karmel that when she became pregnant the second time, living in New York City, she could not understand why the method was not familiar to anyone she sought out, thus making it necessary for her to train herself for her second delivery. After the birth of her second child, Mrs. Karmel's book, *Thank You, Dr. Lamaze*, was published in 1959, recounting her experiences with her two Lamaze deliveries. Although the situation is quite different now, in that the lack of interest in the method which she described in 1959 no longer persists, this book remains today one of the most widely used by expectant mothers and teachers of the Lamaze method.

Mrs. Karmel was also instrumental in organizing a group of interested obstetricians and other professionals into what was to become incorporated, in 1960, as the American Society for Psychoprophylaxis in Obstetrics, usually referred to as ASPO. With the increasing popularity of the method, various chapters of ASPO were created through the U.S., until today ASPO chapters and affiliates may be found in virtually every major city in the country.

Functioning as a nonprofit organization, the society actively continues to encourage and support the use of the method by supplying information to interested parents, hospitals, and professional groups; by sponsoring teacher-training courses for interested professionals; and by making literature, film rentals, teaching aids, etc., available for use by instructors throughout the country.

Even though the United States was relatively late in adopting the use of the Lamaze method, it is amazing to see how popular it has become, with many institutions sponsoring courses of instruction for couples, and every year more and more hospitals allowing husbands and wives to participate together in the labor and delivery rooms.

While much of this advance has been due to doctors and nurses becoming aware of the advantages of the method, much of the increase in popularity of the Lamaze method has come about because of word-of-mouth influence from one couple to another—because of "satisfied customers" telling their friends.

You may ask, "What has Pavlov and his salivating dogs to go with my labor and delivery being a satisfying experience?" The answer is that the Lamaze training falls into two major categories: (1) *deconditioning*: by learning correct information about what labor is really like, you can rid yourself of an accumulation of misinformation you have stored up for years; (2) *conditioning:* you will learn a set pattern of breathing and relaxation techniques, and by being reinforced with daily practice, they will become conditioned responses that will allow you to control your labor rather than having it control you.

When your uterus starts to contract, it will signal your conditioned responses of breathing and relaxing, which will have become strong enough to minimize the perception of the contraction as painful. In addition, you will have gotten your body in shape for labor by specific daily body-building exercises.

If at all possible, you should receive a course of instruction, given by a responsible professional instructor, with an organized group, starting about eight weeks prior to your due date. In addition to the advantage of having the exercises and breathing techniques demonstrated and explained, with a helpful spontaneous exchange of questions and answers, there are many other benefits derived from participating in a group. There, everyone is pregnant—you are comfortable "all in the same boat," and it is very helpful and encouraging to share your hopes (and sometimes your fears and anxieties).

It is possible, however, for you and your husband to train yourselves, if no classroom instruction is available. If you elect to do this, you should first do sufficient reading to become thoroughly familiar with the Lamaze method. Then you should make out a schedule for yourself, listing the dates during that eight-week period when you will begin each individual exercise. Finally, you should practice each session every single day until your labor begins.

Inquire if there is available a tour of the hospital where you are to deliver, so that you can become familiar with where you are to go and what you are to do when labor begins. Do not hesitate to ask questions about their policies and procedures and anything else about their routines that is not clear in your mind.

The following are specific instructions for mothers interested in using the Lamaze method. Each exercise carries with it a discussion of the biological or psychological benefit which can be received:

1. Body-Building Exercises
2. Neuromuscular Control (Concentration-Relaxation) Exercises.
3. General Breathing Techniques.
4. Breathing for Early Labor.
5. Breathing as Labor Progresses.
6. Breathing for Transition.
7. The Second Stage—Expulsion.

BODY-BUILDING EXERCISES

While these exercises are not something you will actually do in labor, they are specifically designed to prepare the parts of your body that will be involved. They are simple, they are few in number, and for the normal, healthy pregnant female, they are in no way harmful. They will also be helpful in preventing or alleviating some of the annoyances and discomforts frequently associated with the last month or two of pregnancy, such as low backaches, leg cramps, and the feeling of heaviness of the abdomen. These exercises will provide a purposeful form of routine daily physical activity, will improve your circulation, and will help to create a sense of well-being.

The body-building exercises should be practiced every day, as many times as your schedule will permit, but no less than five times a day for each exercise. They should be done on the floor with only the softness of a bathmat or scatter rug. For the exercises done in a supine position, a pillow may be placed under the head with a smaller pillow under each knee.

1. *Tailor Sitting*
Sit on the floor cross-legged with your back slightly rounded and relaxed. Sit in this position not only when exercising but

also as often as possible during the routine daily activities that you have been performing sitting in a chair. You will find it quite a comfortable position for such things as reading, watching TV, and sewing or knitting.

If you begin to experience the discomfort of low back strain, sit on the floor in the tailor position. Let your head loosely hang forward and gently rock back and forth until your back is a rounded arch (like a Halloween cat's) to straighten out that hyperaccentuated lordotic curve in your back.

2. *Tailor Stretch*

Sitting on the floor in the tailor position, place the soles of your feet together in front of you and then pull your feet toward the groin, as close to your body as possible. Now take your hands and push your knees down toward the floor. If your feet start to slide away from your body, put your hands on your ankles to hold them in place, and use your elbows to push your knees down toward the floor. At first, the muscles in your thighs may feel uncomfortably tight doing this exercise, but in a few weeks, you should easily be able to pull your feet all the way back to your groin and have your knees loosely go all the way to the floor.

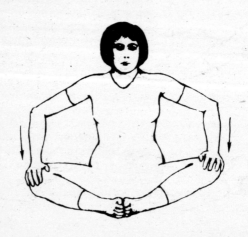

The Lamaze-trained woman who has been doing this exercise for six to eight weeks is then not under an uncomfortable strain when her legs are placed in the stirrups during delivery, or in labor when her obstetrician asks her to separate her legs for examinations.

3. *The Pelvic Rock*

The benefits of this exercise are realized in two areas, the abdomen and the back. When you have progressed to the second, or expulsive, stage of labor, one of the forces you will use to help the uterine contraction in pushing your baby out of the birth canal is the tightening of the abdominal muscles. Most likely, during pregnancy, these muscles have been allowed to become lax and by now have lost tone. This exercise will help to improve that muscle tone and allow you to work more effectively during the "pushing" stage of labor. Since it straightens the curve in your back, it will also be helpful in preventing low back pain.

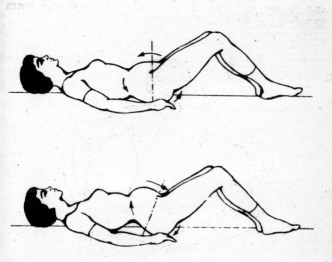

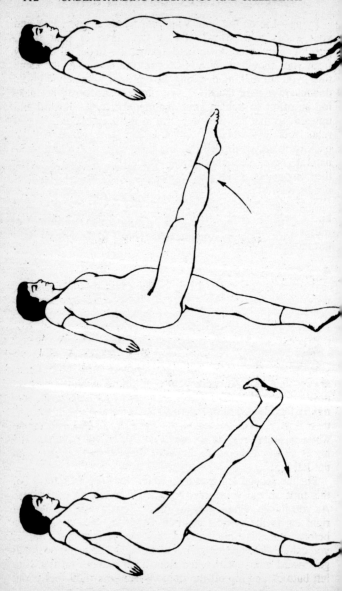

Lying—Lie on the floor with your hands at your sides and your knees bent. Slowly flatten the curve in your back, pushing your spine down hard against the floor, all the way from your shoulders to your coccyx (tail bone). At the same time, you are rocking or tilting the bones of your pelvic girdle downward toward the floor, you should consciously be making an effort to tighten your abdominal muscles inward and upward, so that they become firm to the touch. Then, as you relax your abdominal musculature, the bony pelvis will go back to the relaxed position, and your back will return to its natural curve. Remember, the ''tilting'' of the pelvis means the bony pelvis, inside, and the fatty part of the buttocks must not be raised up, but remain on the floor.

Standing—Stand erect with your feet flat on the floor and knees slightly bent. Arch back, then contract abdominal muscles, rolling hips back to standing position. Repeat until the motion is smooth.

4. Leg Exercises

Another of the discomforts of the latter months of pregnancy is leg cramps. Maybe you have already had the unpleasant experience of a painful charley horse in your calf. Unfortunately, these often increase rather than decrease as the pregnancy progresses.

This exercise is done lying on the floor with the hands at your sides. With your toes pointed and with both knees always kept straight, raise your right leg to as high a vertical position as is possible. Then, with your foot high in the air, tightly flex the ankle so it is at a 45-degree angle with the leg, then slowly lower the leg to the floor. It is helpful to inhale while raising the leg to the vertical position and exhale as the leg is slowly lowered to the floor. Repeat the exercise with the left leg.

For the second leg exercise, lie on the floor as before, but this time spread your arms out at right angles to your body. As you inhale, again with the toes pointed, raise the straight right leg to the vertical position as before; flex the ankle as before. But this time, instead of lowering it to the floor as you exhale, let your leg go out to the right side as far as it will go toward your outstretched right hand without raising your left buttock and hip off the floor. When your right foot is out toward your hand as far as possible, you should feel a stretch of the muscles of the inside of the thigh and the right lower quadrant of the abdominal wall.

Now point the right toes again, inhale as you raise the straight right leg back to the vertical position; flex the ankle and exhale as you slowly let your heel go back to the floor.

Repeat with the left leg.

5. *Getting Up*

As the pregnancy progresses and the size of the abdomen increases, the pregnant woman feels more and more clumsy when arising from an awkward position. In such instances, you will find that using your hands and feet as levers is very helpful.

For example, when lying flat on the floor, turn onto your right side; place your left palm down on the floor in front of your face and push up with it, using it as a lever to raise the top half of your body to a sitting position. Then push with your left hand, with your knees bent, to raise the rest of your body from the floor.

6. *Posture*

In addition to the routine daily practice of the above exercises, you should now also pay more attention to your posture, particularly when standing or walking. As your pregnancy progresses and the uterus enlarges, the weight tends to pull the abdomen forward and the curve in the lower back is sometimes greatly accentuated into a swayback. This is largely responsible for low backaches late in pregnancy, and you should make a conscious effort to "think tall" as you walk or stand, so as to straighten out that hyperaccentuated curve in your back.

7. *Resting*

The best rest is achieved by lying down, not sitting. Never sit when you can lie down. Put a piece of plywood under your mattress. Lie on your back with one pillow under your head and another under your knees. When you wish to get up out of bed, gently roll over on your abdomen and slide out of bed onto your knees. Never jerk or force your back to rotate rapidly or forcibly.

When sleeping, do not lie on your stomach. When you lie on your side, draw up both knees. Keep your arms below your shoulders during the night, preferably in a relaxed position along the sides of the body.

8. *Lifting Things*

Squat down directly in front of any object you plan to lift, including a baby. Get as close as possible, then stand up slowly while firmly holding the object tightly to your body and letting the legs—not the back—do the work. Never lift while bending forward, as in taking something out of the trunk of a car. Do not lean over furniture to open or close windows. The main point is that you should never lift with your legs straight. In addition, never work or lift with your arms higher than your shoulders or lower than your waist. Do not jerk or force open a drawer.

9. *Sitting*

Sit in a straight chair with a firm back. Avoid low, soft chairs or lounges that allow you to sink deep down into the upholstery. You can hurt your back when getting up on your feet. Never sit more than 15 minutes at a time; get up and move about frequently. Let your feet rest on a low stool so that your knees are higher than your hips. This position relaxes your back.

10. *Standing and Walking*

Watch your feet when climbing up and down stairs, over curbs, and walking on rocky or rough ground. You must take care to avoid stumbles and sudden jerks to your back. Open doors widely enough to walk through comfortably. Never stand in the same position for more than a minute. Shift from one foot to the other so that your weight is not on the same leg and foot for longer than a minute. A little footstool or box that supports one foot or the other, in turn, is comforting to the back.

11. *Driving*

Push the car seat forward so that your knees are higher than your hips. Snugly fasten the safety belt and shoulder harness; they support your body and back and prevent a sudden twist if there is an emergency stop, turn, or bump.

12. *House and Garden*

Get down on your knees to do jobs that otherwise would make you strain your back to reach. If your back is really hurting, do not vacuum or make beds.

13. *Relaxing Your Back*

The simplest and safest way to relax your back is to stand in a hot shower directed against your back, or to soak in a warm tub two or three times every day. Gentle but thorough exercises relax and strengthen back muscles.

NEUROMUSCULAR CONTROL (CONTRACTION-RELAXATION EXERCISES)

This is the most important aspect of the teamwork training of the couple who will be working together in labor. In fact, this entire portion of your training might well be primarily directed toward your husband, since he is the one who will be responsible for your state of relaxation during labor.

Anyone would probably agree on the importance of being able to relax during labor. Even if you have never had any firsthand contact with someone having a baby, you can imagine how much easier labor can be if the woman remains completely relaxed.

Research shows that relaxed mothers who are less anxious during labor and delivery have shorter labors and deliver babies with high Apgar scores (measures infant's respiration, color, heartbeat, and reflexes). Relaxation not only shortens your labor but helps a woman conserve her energy by preventing the fear-tension pain cycle, ensures oxygen supply to her and the fetus, decreases her pain, and above all else, allows her contractions to be effective.

Tensing during childbirth is a natural response to the tensing of the uterus. However, tension not only causes exhaustion, oxygen depletion, and a lower pain threshold, but actually prolongs labor physiologically. The hormone that causes your uterus to contract is oxytocin. Adrenaline, the hormone that accompanies the tension fear-pain syndrome, actually inhibits the effects of oxytoxin and makes your contractions less effective.

Relaxing for labor, however, is different from ordinary relaxation. For example, while the housewife is doing her daily chores, she may decide to "sit down, have a cup of coffee, and relax." This is a passive, let-it-happen type of relaxation, which is generally adequate for refreshing the housewife. It is fine—as far as it goes.

During labor, however, one needs more. The laboring woman should be able to employ a make-it-happen type of relaxation—and you can learn to make it happen—by concentrating on the body parts you want to be relaxed, even while other body parts are tight. By daily practice, you can condition yourself to relax this way.

Even the totally untrained woman in labor is admonished by the doctors and nurses in attendance to "just relax," and at the end of each contraction, she may try, but before the let-it-happen type of relaxation can be effective, another contraction begins, and she lets the tightening uterine muscles cause her entire body to become tense.

Anyone who has worked in a labor room can describe some of the mothers' reactions to the onset of a uterine contraction. With the beginning tightening of the uterine muscles, she thinks, "Here it comes," and she may clench her fists or squeeze the side rails of the bed, so that her fingernails are digging into the palms of her hands, and her arms become completely rigid all the way up. Sometimes she will be seen curling her toes tightly downward, as she tightens her ankles and knees, until her legs become rigid. Sometimes she will be seen clenching her teeth so that her jaws and neck muscles are rigidly outstanding. She seems to be bracing herself for combat with the uterine contraction, as if by this bracing she could prevent contraction.

Of course, the uterus must forcibly contract in labor. It would be undesirable for the uterus not to contract. This contracting force pushes the baby downward and retracts the cervix from the baby's head. But if, when the uterus starts to contract, other muscle groups and other body parts also tighten up in a follow-the-leader fashion, it is extremely wasteful; it is wasteful use of energy she will need later on for pushing in the second stage of labor; it is wasteful burning of oxygen that should be going to oxygenate her baby; and the end result is nonproductive fatigue.

In contrast, the Lamaze-trained mother who has learned the make-it-happen type of relaxation, having practiced it daily with her husband, with daily strengthening of her conditioned response, can be relaxed throughout labor, not only between contractions, but during them.

In order for you to realize maximum benefit from your relaxation efforts, this is one group of exercises that *must* be practiced every day (as subtle as it is, the process of conditioning is taking place daily) and *must* be practiced while your husband (or some substitute coach) is at home to direct you and to check on your progress. Of course, during the day, you may want to do some extra practice to speed up the learning process, but at least once a day, be sure to go through all of the steps of relaxing, with your husband directing the practice. For one reason, when you are practicing without your coach, it is extremely difficult for you to correctly appraise your own state of relaxation. For another, in active labor, it would probably be your husband who would first notice any signs of tension beginning before you would be aware of them yourself.

At first, the relaxation exercises may seem very time-consuming and very difficult because you have never experienced this type or degree of relaxation, and in the beginning, you do not know what sensation you are looking for. Just try to keep in mind that, as you do them day after day, your body is learning to respond when your husband gives the command to relax, and by conditioning, that response will continue to increase. Then, in labor, when your husband perceives that you are starting to become tense and he tells you to relax, you will be able to let your entire body go completely limp. This ability will be invaluable to you in labor!

Practice Exercises for Relaxation

1. Lie on the floor with your hands relaxed at your sides. If you like, you may place pillows under your head and knees. Before your husband begins testing your extremities, make a conscious effort to let your body "go loose." You may have heard of the recommendation given to insomniacs to help them fall asleep. It is said that if you start at the top of the head and, step by step,

consciously think of relaxing every part of your body, you will be asleep by the time you get to your toes.

2. At your husband's command, "Contract your right arm," you will make a fist, raise the tightened, outstretched arm a few inches off the floor, and keep it up this way until your husband has time to check successively the relaxation of the joints and muscles of your left arm and your right and left legs to see that they are perfectly limp before he gives the command to release the right arm.

3. Continue as above until you have done all the following exercises, with your husband giving the commands to contract each specific area and then checking the state of relaxation of all other areas before he says, "Release."

Contract left arm (check relaxation)—Release.

Contract right leg (check relaxation)—Release.

Contract left leg (check relaxation)—Release.

Contract right arm and right leg (check relaxation)—Release.

Contract both arms (check relaxation)—Release.

Contract both legs (check relaxation)—Release.

Contract right arm and left leg (check relaxation)—Release.

Contract left arm and right leg (check relaxation)—Release.

To the husbands: You can greatly assist the learning process by your verbal directions "Relax," "Let go," "Let your arm and leg slowly sink downward," "Let me have the weight of the extremity in my hand," etc. Vocally, you are helping your wife sharpen the focus of her concentration. Begin these verbal directions with the joints (i.e., "Relax your shoulder, elbow, knee," etc.) because they are the easiest for her to relax. She already had voluntary control of joints, and without any conscious thought, she uses this control when, for example, she bends her knees to walk up steps, or bends her elbow to take a bite of food. When you see the joints are relaxed, then proceed to give her the verbal directions "Let all the muscles in your arm (or leg) go limp in my hand." As she gradually learns to let go, you will feel the weight of the extremity in your hand slowly and gradually increasing, and when you let go of it, the arm or leg should plop, falling to the floor as a dead weight.

When you first start to practice, it may take several minutes to go through the entire process of relaxing all extremities. But as her learning (conditioning) increases, the time spent will grow less and less each day, and by the time labor begins, it will just take one command (without these extra verbal instructions) to have her relax her entire body, even though at the same time the uterine muscles may be tightly contracting.

Again, let me stress how important this ability will be to you in labor, especially when you get to the transition phase when the mother's ability to relax is strongly challenged.

GENERAL BREATHING TECHNIQUES

One of the most important parts of your Lamaze training is the method of breathing used in labor, which will enable you to stay in control of your uterine contractions. Before you start to learn any of the Lamaze breathing techniques, you should read again the parts of this book that deal with the anatomy and physiology of labor (Chapter 7). You should learn what to expect as signs of the onset of labor and study how the course of labor can get a clearer picture of how (and when) your Lamaze techniques are to be employed.

For the sake of brevity here, let us just refer to the longest part of labor, Stage I, as the "cervical dilatation stage," and the shorter Stage II as the "expulsion stage." It is throughout Stage I that you will be using your Lamaze breathing methods to control discomfort, changing from one technique to another as your contractions increase in intensity.

At the very onset of labor, contractions are almost always mild, usually occurring at irregular intervals and frequently are spaced wide apart. Many women describe them as "crampy" in nature, and they probably will not require you to begin any of your special breathing techniques. When asked, "When should I start to use my Lamaze breathing?" the rule of thumb used by most ASPO teachers is that no Lamaze breathing will be necessary "as long as you can comfortably walk and talk throughout a contraction." It would be wasteful for you to confine yourself to a regime when none is really necessary. This would only make the period when it is necessary seem longer to you.

When your Lamaze breathing becomes necessary, you will first use a slow, rhythmic, deep-chest breathing, inhaling through your nose and exhaling through pursed lips at a rate of approximately 6 to 9 times a minute.

When this first technique is no longer effective in controlling your discomfort, you will switch to the second type, a shallow panting, which should start slowly but accelerate in rate as your contraction increases to a peak, then decelerate as the contraction fades away.

You will continue to use this accelerating-decelerating panting throughout the cervical-dilatation stage of labor, but as the second (expulsive) stage approaches, when the baby's head is lower in the pelvis, most women feel a sensation of pressure in the rectal area and have an "urge to bear down." Then they need a new type of "transition" breathing (panting interspersed with blowing out) in order to control this urge until the cervix is fully dilated, and their doctor has instructed them to start pushing.

When full dilatation of the cervix is achieved, the expulsive Stage II of your labor will begin and later on in this chapter, we will discuss the proper method to be used in helping to push your baby through the birth canal.

When you are ready to start your daily practice breathing (approximately eight weeks before your due date), there are some additional activities that should be included since they are to be incorporated into *all* of your Lamaze breathing techniques:

1. *Take a deep, cleansing breath*, before and after each minute of practicing each type of breathing. Even though these cleansing breaths may seem the same as the deep-chest breathing you will be doing in the early part of labor, start right at the beginning to establish the habit of taking an extra cleansing breath before and after each minute of practice. When you get further on into labor, using the panting breathing, or during the pushing stage, these extra "deep, cleansing breaths" will serve you well.

2. *Effleurage:* When the uterine muscles inside your body are contracting, there is also a tightening of the muscles and ligaments that surround and are attached to the uterus. At the height of a contraction, even the skin over the abdomen is taut. Effleurage is using your hands in a slow, gentle, light massage of the abdomen, which will feel good when all of these tissues are tightly contracted.

In order to control the rate at which your hands travel over the skin of the abdomen, start doing this massage with your first slow breathing, which is done at a rate of about 6 to 9 times a minute. Starting at the lower part of your abdomen, as you inhale, bring your hands gently up to the top, and as you exhale slowly let them go back down your abdomen. If you establish this pattern and rate early in your practice, you will then not be inclined to let your hands also speed up when you start doing the panting breathing and your husband says, "Accelerate." It would not feel good—in fact, it would probably be an irritating nuisance—if your hands were to increase at the same rate as your panting breathing.

3. *Focus your eyes.* Pick one spot (on the wall, the ceiling, or the floor), and do not let your eyes wander from that one place.

At first, you may feel that you look ridiculous staring at one spot as you do your breathing, but this foolish feeling will soon go away, and you will lose any self-consciousness which might be present in the beginning. This focus of your eyes is simply another area of concentration. There are almost always distracting influences present when you are in labor, visual as well as auditory. You should condition yourself not to be concerned with the sights and sounds that do not pertain to your labor, such as traffic in the street outside, a stretcher going down the hall, or personnel coming in and going out of your room.

This is one day when you should be entirely self-centered.

Your sphere—"your little corner of the world"—should consist only of your contraction, your activi-

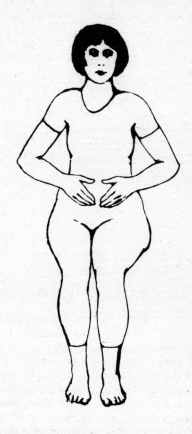

ties in response to that contraction, and your husband's voice telling you what to do. Therefore, when you pick out one spot to look at, you are less likely to let your mind wander, following your wandering eyes.

4. *"Contraction begins"* should be said *aloud* each time you begin a minute of practice breathing, and "Contraction ends" should be said aloud as the minute ends.

Most of the time, you will be practicing with your husband, and he should say aloud, "Contraction begins," but even if you are practicing alone, you should say it aloud to yourself. This may seem a little strange to say words aloud when there is only you and the clock and no one else present to hear. But *you* are hearing it! —that is the important thing. You hear the words, and you respond by starting to do your breathing, beginning your effleurage, focusing your eyes, etc. This is your response to the stimulus of the spoken words.

Remember the earlier mention of the Pavlovian conditioning utilized in the Lamaze method. The words "Contraction begins" are the stimulus, albeit a secondary stimulus, but nonetheless the stimulus to which you will respond by beginning your planned activities. When labor begins and the actual contraction, the primary stimulus, occurs, you will automatically begin to do these activities to which you have become conditioned.

A word to husbands: It is also helpful if you will call aloud when 15 seconds have passed, then 30 seconds, then 45 seconds, and finally one minute. For some unknown psychological reason, the minute seems much shorter when it is chopped up into smaller parts. These announcements of the passing seconds will also be encouraging milestones, so that she will know that she is "getting somewhere," that progress is actually taking place and that this one contraction is not going to last until she is old and gray. Remember, one of the most important functions of the husband in labor is to keep his wife apprised of any and every sign of progress.

Every day, you should do your practice breathing in the three positions you will be in during labor: (1) sitting up in a chair; (2) standing; (3) in a semireclining position (not absolutely flat), propped up in bed, with pillows supporting your back and shoulders.

Then in labor, when you are at home sitting in a chair or riding to the hospital in a car, you will be accustomed to breathing in this sitting position.

If a contraction begins when you are walking from the car into the hospital or standing at the admission desk waiting to go to the labor suite, it will not be the first time you have ever done your breathing in a standing position.

The semireclining position is the one you will probably use the most after you are in the labor room at the hospital. The head of the labor bed should be raised to a comfortable level and one or two pillows used to give additional support to your back and shoulders.

It will give you an added sense of security to have repeatedly practiced your breathing in all three positions. Then, no situation you are in will be new or strange or unrehearsed when labor begins.

BREATHING FOR EARLY LABOR

As mentioned before, the cramplike, irregular contractions announcing the onset of labor will probably not require any special breathing technique. However, when those contractions have established themselves in a regular, rhythmic pattern and have started to increase in frequency, duration, and intensity (namely, when you can no longer comfortably walk and talk throughout a contraction), you will start to use a rhythmic, slow, deep-chest breathing at a rate of 6 to 9 times per minute.

Although this breathing is simple, easy to do, and in no way demanding or exhausting, it will (a) initiate the process of concentration, and (b) serve as a method of controlled relaxation.

In some ways, this first breathing technique reminds me of a sigh. As you know, we all have the natural, built-in phenomenon called a sigh, which we employ without even thinking about it whenever there is a need to relax. When you are tired or angry or just exasperated by some minor aggravation, do you not find yourself using the deep, slow inhalation-exhalation of a sigh as a means of relaxing?

For some women, this slow chest breathing is adequate for more than half of their labor; for others, it is helpful only during the early part of the first stage, until the cervix is 3 or 4 centimeters dilated. In any event, you should use it as long as it is effective for you, whether that be for only two or three contractions, or for two or three hours, or for much longer.

Practice for Early Labor

1. Take a deep, cleansing breath.
2. At your husband's command, "Contraction begins," start slowly to inhale through your nose, to the full capacity of your lungs, then slowly let the air out through your pursed lips in a controlled exhalation.
3. Repeat 6 to 9 times a minute. Have your husband count the number of breaths you are taking so that you can achieve this rate. Also, he should say aloud when 15 seconds, 30 seconds, 45 seconds, and 60 seconds have passed, before he says "Contraction ends."
4. Add the effleurage—bring your cupped hands lightly and slowly up around over the outside of the abdomen as you inhale and then down the middle of your abdomen as you exhale.
5. Take a deep, cleansing breath at the end of the contraction.
6. Repeat in the sitting, standing, and semireclining positions.

Let me stress that this, and all the other Lamaze breathing techniques used in the first stage of labor, should be chest breathing. You should not use your diaphragm and abdominal muscles until you get to the "pushing" required in the second stage. There is enough happening in the abdominal and pelvic areas during your contractions, and it is better not to exert any extra pressure on the already irritable uterus.

BREATHING AS LABOR PROGRESSES

When the slow deep-chest breathing is no longer effective (regardless of the amount of time that has passed or the number of centimeters your cervix has dilated), you will switch to a shallow, superficial panting breathing. This usually occurs after 5 to 6 centimeters of dilatation.

In labor, you will start to pant slowly, since the beginning of a contraction is mild, and the rate of your panting will increase as the contraction builds in intensity, up to a peak. You will maintain the rapid rate throughout the peak of the contraction and start to decelerate only when the contraction starts to subside.

For your first week of practice panting, however, do not

concern yourself with speed. That will come more easily later on, when you have mastered the technique of panting smoothly, evenly, regularly, and without great effort, so that at the end of a minute, you could easily have kept going longer if your husband had not said "Contraction ends."

For most women, it takes a full week just to learn how to pant this way, and it is a rare instance when the couple should proceed to rapid acceleration before the first week is up. Do not let your enthusiasm cause you to lose sight of long-term goals. Therefore, schedule yourself for a week of practice panting at any rate that is comfortable for you, and aim at achieving a rhythmic, metronome-like regularity rather than trying to increase your speed the first week.

This panting is done with the mouth slightly open, and it is sometimes helpful if you can hear the sound of your breathing so as to ensure the same amount of air going in and out with each exhalation. *It is imperative that there is an equal amount of air being exchanged in the inhalation and the exhalation.* Otherwise, you would not be able to continue for the full minute (much less learn to speed up for the peak).

There are two common errors that could prevent your accomplishing a full minute's worth of panting by the end of one week's time: (1) If you take in more air as you inhale than you are letting out when you exhale, you may soon start to feel a light-headedness which is a sign of hyperventilation. If, during a minute of practice, you experience any dizziness or a tingling sensation in your fingers or toes, you will know that you must readjust the amount of air you are inhaling so that it corresponds to the amount you are exhaling. (2) Just the reverse of the above, if you are blowing off more air with each exhalation than you are taking in with each inhalation, it means that you are borrowing some air from the reserve air that always stays in your lungs. Soon your lungs will just not let you borrow any more without demanding a repayment, and you will have to stop the shallow panting to take in a deep breath to replace the air in your lungs before you can continue panting.

Therefore, if you continue to have difficulty reaching the end of a minute's practice panting, you (or your husband) should try to identify which of these two errors you are committing. You can then correct the problem by carefully listening to your breathing and making a conscious effort to regulate the flow of air in and out.

Practice Panting for First Week

1. Take a deep, cleansing breath.
2. At your husband's command "Contraction begins," start to inhale-exhale in short, shallow, superficial pants, keeping your mouth open and your teeth slightly parted, always being aware of equal amounts of air going in and out.
3. Continue for one minute (without regard for speed) until your husband says, "Contraction ends." As he is timing the contraction, he should announce when 15, 30, 45, and 60 seconds have passed.
4. Take another deep, cleansing breath.
5. Repeat in sitting, standing, and semireclining positions.
6. When you can easily pant for one full minute, add the effleurage.

Practice Panting for Subsequent Weeks

1. Take a deep, cleansing breath.
2. At your husband's command "Contraction begins," start the shallow-superficial panting at a slow rate, and try to imagine that your uterine muscles are just beginning to contract.
3. As your imaginary contraction begins to increase in intensity and your husband says, "Fifteen seconds, accelerate," start to make the panting faster (but shallower). Continue to increase your speed as you imagine the contraction rising to a peak and your husband announces, "Thirty seconds." Keep this accelerated speed sustained throughout the imagined peak and then start to slow down when your husband announces, "Forty-five seconds, decelerate." Gradually slow your panting down to the rate you were breathing when the contraction began, by the time your husband says, "Sixty seconds, contraction ends."
4. Take a deep, cleansing breath.
5. Repeat in the sitting, standing, and semireclining position.

6. When you can easily and comfortably accelerate and decelerate at your husband's commands, add the effleurage.

At the beginning of practice panting, you will probably have to make a concerted, conscious effort to keep this just chest breathing, and you should watch to see that the abdomen does not move. At first, you will see movement at about the level of your breasts, but gradually, as you become more proficient, the panting will become more and more shallow. After a few weeks, you will see that your chest seems to stay almost still, and the only movement will be very high, in the hollow just below your throat at the top of your breast-bone.

This accelerated-decelerated panting is usually the most effective Lamaze breathing technique in controlling the discomfort of your contractions, and it will probably be used over a longer period of time than any other type of breathing. By the same token, it is more exacting, it requires greater concentration and more effort than the deep-chest breathing previously described. Therefore, it would be wasteful and tiring for you to begin rapid panting with your first mild contractions, or when it is not really necessary—when the slow breathing would be adequate.

On the other hand, do not hold off beginning panting breathing for any certain time interval, or for any specific amount of cervical dilatation to be achieved, by some stoic attitude of "I will grit my teeth and bear it." This is not an endurance test. You will simply begin the panting breathing whenever the slow deep-chest breathing is no longer effective in the control of your contractions.

Remember, you are the one to determine what breathing is suitable for you at any given time during your labor. Whatever works for you is what you should be using.

If you are not able to receive any classroom instructions or participate in any group sessions, start your daily practice breathing about eight weeks before your due date and allow the following spacing in your schedule for beginning your practice:

1. Practice the slow, deep-chest breathing with effleurage for one week before you add the panting breathing.
2. Take a full week to learn how to do the panting breathing before you concern yourself with accelerating the rate.

3. Do a week of practicing the accelerating-decelerating panting and add the effleurage before you go on to the transition breathing.

When you start to practice the panting breathing, you may notice a slightly bothersome dryness of the mouth. After a while, this will diminish somewhat as you become more proficient in your technique, because your jaws and facial muscles will become more relaxed and you will salivate more. It may, however, still be something of a problem when you use the panting during labor, since this is open-mouth breathing. To alleviate this, you should take with you to the labor room a small bag (i.e., brown kraft bag from the grocery store) containing the following articles:

1. A chapstick to keep your lips from feeling dry and cracked.
2. A good supply of sour, tart (lemon or lime, not chocolate) lollipops to suck on between contractions (or a whole lemon if that suits your taste and your doctor doesn't mind). The tartness will cause you to salivate and the lollipops will also provide some sugar.
3. A small bottle of mouthwash to freshen your mouth.

The bag should be small enough so that with the edges folded down, it will be the size that will just cover your mouth and nose. Then, should you feel any light-headedness or signs of hyperventilation during your labor, you can breathe into the brown bag and by rebreathing your own exhaled carbon dioxide clear up the hyperventilation.

You can put into the bag any other small items you think you will need in labor. You should carry it in your hand rather than putting it in your suitcase since in most hospitals, your suitcase will be taken directly to your postpartum room, and you will probably not have it with you in the labor suite. You may want to include some talcum powder to sprinkle over your abdomen as you are doing the effleurage. Also, take along a thick washcloth (since many hospitals use disposable washcloths) so that, if you feel hot and sweaty during transition, you can wet it with cold water and wash your face and neck to cool off.

BREATHING FOR TRANSITION

The dictionary defines the word "transition" as "the passage from one place, state, stage of development, to another." Before describing the transition breathing, let us take a minute to see how that definition applies to your progressing labor.

You may have spent several hours in reaching this point, starting with those first irregular "cramps," which become regular, cyclic contractions that become progressively longer and stronger as the intervals between become shorter. The time and effort spent in labor thus far has been for one purpose—the effacement and dilatation of the cervix, the opening of the mouth of the uterus so that your baby can pass through the birth canal.

Now you are almost at the end of that long Stage I (the dilatation stage), and you are almost at the beginning of the shorter Stage II (the expulsion stage).

This transition phase, then, by definition, simply means that you are passing from one major stage of labor into another. But to you, in labor, it will probably mean much more because several new things may start to happen—and seemingly all at once:

1. *Contractions:* After the onset of active labor, contractions usually maintain a rhythmic, cyclic pattern until transition is reached. Now they will probably become longer in duration and stronger in intensity, but what is more disconcerting is that they may assume an erratic character that makes them unpredictable in length, strength, or frequency. You may have less time between contractions to rest, and contractions may rise quickly to the peak so that you have to start your acceleration earlier and maintain the acceleration throughout a longer peak before it starts to wane.

2. *Tremors:* I am sure that at some time in your life, through fatigue or tension, you have experienced tremors of your extremities. When you tried in a determined fashion to hold that extremity still, it would shake even harder.

Presumably by practicing your neuromuscular-control

exercises every day and learning how to relax on command, these tremors can be avoided in labor. However, if they do occur, it should not be alarming to you—it is a fairly common occurrence in transition. You will simply use your relaxation techniques to make them go away, rather than trying to use force to hold the extremity still.

Let me say here that transition is a time in labor when the husband has to be most alert to any signs of tension building up in his wife. With all the activity that is going on inside her body, it is very easy for her to allow these strong contractions to lead her into a state of tension unless the husband is constantly alert to keeping her relaxed.

3. *Temperature changes:* At this time, the mother may complain of extreme temperature changes, and strangely enough, she may feel either very hot or very cold. In either case, the treatment is symptomatic. If she is cold, ask the nurse for more cover. If she is uncomfortably warm and sweating, take a large washcloth and wet it with cold water to wipe her face and neck to cool her off.

4. *Bloody show:* The same type of bloodstained mucous discharge that you saw on the onset of labor will again be present, only now in larger quantities.

5. *Nausea and vomiting:* If there is a tendency for the mother to feel nauseated during labor, it is usually during transition that this will occur. This is especially true if she has unwisely eaten a heavy meal after labor began, believing it would give her added strength for labor, or fearing that she would be hungry in labor, knowing that no food or drink would be allowed once she entered the hospital.

6. *Irritability:* During this period, the mother may sometimes become very cross and ill-tempered, so shrewish and cantankerous that the husband may be made to feel that none of his attempts to aid or comfort her are in the right direction. If the husband realizes that this is a very usual occurrence, he will not be dissuaded by her agitation, or shy away from his duties as coach and director, but will realize that the reassurance of his

presence is more important than ever. Therefore, instead of "leaving her alone" as she might suggest, he can usually be more helpful by making his instructions to her even stronger and more forceful.

Sometimes in class, women who are in their second or third pregnancy and have returned for a refresher course will try to describe their own mental state during the transition phase of their previous labors. It seems that there is some nebulous quality to it that is hard to verbalize. They use phrases such as: "I would forget what I was supposed to do next," or "Even though I hadn't any medication, I felt kind of like I was drugged," and one mother, for lack of a better description said, "I don't know what it is, you just get a little crazy." This transient loss of perspective and lack of direction (and purpose) require that the husband take a good firm grip on the control of the situation until this brief time passes. And it is brief!

These "side effects" may also appear accentuated because they occur during the most active part of your labor. They can seem grossly exaggerated because it is during this period when you will be working the hardest to concentrate and stay in complete control of your uterine contractions—when you are perhaps tiring, both physically and mentally, if your labor has been a long one—and when you would least like to have any "extras" to distract you. It is a time when so much is going on that, alas, everything seems exaggerated.

For instance, if you were not in labor (or even pregnant) but had just been involved in some active physical sport and felt a tremor in one of your extremities, it would probably not be alarming to you. You would probably just take a minute or two to relax and allow the easing of tension to bring the shaking to a stop. Or if you were doing some hard physical work and you began to feel very warm and to sweat, it would not frighten you. You would just try to think of something that could help you to cool off, such as washing your face and neck with a cool cloth. Therefore, why not do the same thing in labor?

If one (or more) of these annoyances comes along with the transition phase, try to think, "How would I deal with this if

I were not in labor?" Such thinking can serve to improve your perspective and may be helpful in allowing these minor "crisis" periods to pass quickly.

Even though transition is apt to be the most difficult period of your entire labor, you should not approach this period with fear or dread. Instead, you should think of this as the most welcome milestone you will have reached. What a landmark! What a sense of accomplishment when you realize that the long and tedious first stage of your labor will soon be finished. Soon, now, your doctor will examine you and say that your cervix is fully dilated and it is time for you to help push your baby out into the world. It is true that during transition, both you and your husband will have to work very hard to keep you in control, but along with that hard work comes the exciting realization that you will soon give birth.

Throughout your labor, up to now, any signs of progress, any milestone reached had to come from either your doctor or your husband as they announced the amount of cervical dilation you had achieved. To you, it probably was painstakingly slow. But now, when you experience the "urge to bear down" that comes with transition, you have your own firsthand, tangible realization that your baby will soon be born.

It is this urge to bear down, with the feeling of pressure in the rectal area, that gives rise to the need for another change in your Lamaze breathing.

As your uterine muscles have contracted, and as the cervix has retracted, your baby's head has moved farther downward in the pelvis, so that in transition, you will probably feel a sensation of pressure caused by the head pressing on the rectum and a feeling of wanting to move your bowels. This urge can become quite strong, so much so that even heavily medicated women will sometimes be roused by it and insist that they "have to go to the bathroom."

As soon as the cervix is fully dilated, and you are in the second stage of labor, that urge will be your signal to start pushing, using your efforts to augment the uterine contractions to help your baby through the birth canal. However, until the cervix is fully dilated, any pushing efforts on your part would be just wasted energy—you cannot "push the cervix open." Furthermore, it is believed that pushing before dilatation is complete can be harmful to the cervix by causing edema (swelling) and possibly even tearing of tissue.

Therefore, the purpose of a different type of breathing for transition is to counteract the urge to bear down until your doctor tells you it is time to start pushing, and the way to accomplish this is forcibly to blow out whenever the urge appears. This blowing of air should not be a slow, long-drawn-out expulsion of air, but rather a quick, forceful, explosive, staccato blowing with which you will feel a tightening of your abdominal muscles. Purse your lips as if you were going to say the letter ''O,'' and your cheeks will puff out just as the air is trying to escape your pursed lips. If you are having problems doing this, I suggest that you imagine a large lighted candle situated approximately two feet from your face which you have to blow out with one quick expulsion of air.

You can test what effect this blowing out will have on the pressure in the rectal area by sitting in a chair (or on the toilet) with your feet flat on the floor, straining downward as if you were constipated and trying to have a bowel movement, and then quickly blowing out. There is a feeling of release, of ''letting go,'' in the rectal area as soon as the air starts to escape your lips. You will find it is impossible to continue straining downward in the rectal area while you are ''straining'' with your abdominal muscles and diaphragm to expel the air from your lungs.

In labor, when the times comes that you will need this blowing out, you will be using your accelerated panting breathing to control your contractions, and so the next step in your practice will be to learn to incorporate the blowing out into your breathing, without disturbing the rate of rhythm of your panting—without having it ''throw you off.'' You can do this by establishing a rhythmic pattern of pant-blow, using six pants and then allowing the blowing out to consume the time that would be required for the next two pants.

When you have been practicing this rhythmic pant-blow breathing for a week, you should easily be able to switch from panting to blowing out, and back to panting again, without disturbing the rate of rhythm of your panting. It may be well for you to consider this a practice week, of just learning how to pant-blow, the same way you took a week to learn how to pant before you started trying to accelerate your panting speed.

When this rhythmic pattern of pant-blow breathing has become easy for you to do, you will start practicing the transition breathing in a slightly different fashion, in preparation for the way it will probably be used most effectively in labor. Near the end of the first stage, when the urge to bear down becomes strong and persistent, more than one blowing respiration will probably be required to dispel the urge, so that, in the midst of your panting, you will start to blow out whenever you feel the urge begin. You will repeatedly blow out until the urge goes away, and then you will automatically switch back to your panting rhythm.

In the successive weeks, then, your practice for transition breathing, with your husband calling the commands and timing your contractions, should simulate this sequence of events. The two of you will begin the minute of accelerating panting the same as you have previously learned it, but at some point (or two or three) in the contraction, your husband will say, "Urge," suggesting the beginning of the rectal pressure. You will now blow out repeatedly until he says, "Stop" or "Urge ends," whereupon you will immediately return to panting at whatever rate is necessary to control that phase of the contraction. (*Note to husbands:* This urge does not usually occur in the opening few seconds of the contractions when the uterine muscles are just beginning to tighten up.)

Even though you have progressed to this more sophisticated version of breathing practice for transition, do not abandon your daily practice of this rhythmic pattern of six pant-blow outs. This is a very handy little extra technique to have with you throughout labor, and you may especially want to revert to it when your doctor tells you to stop pushing, just as your baby is being born.

THE SECOND STAGE—EXPULSION

Now that the cervix is fully dilated, you are, at last, ready for the expulsion of your baby through the birth canal. It would seem that even though we refer to this as the second stage of *labor*, one might just as properly call it *birth*, since this is what is actually happening—your baby is ready to leave your womb and make his way into the world. This is a good time for you to turn again to the pages of this book that describe the details of labor (Chapter 7) to review the mechanisms of the second stage of labor and the way your baby moves out the birth canal. Although this second stage is, in a sense, a continuation of what has gone before, it is distinctly different; it is true that uterine contractions continue to occur, but they are now performing a different function, and, for you, they take on a different character.

The work you do in the second stage will probably require the greatest physical effort of your entire labor. In contrast to earlier labor, it requires "more brawn than brain." During these contractions, you will use your entire body to augment the efforts of the uterus, and you will assume the proper posture to facilitate the passage of your baby out of the birth canal.

If it is so important to learn to push correctly, what happens when the mother is heavily medicated or completely "knocked out" by the time the second stage arrives? The answer, of course, is that the baby will be born even though the mother is heavily sedated. The uterus will just have to do all of the work by itself, and it will take a much longer time. The duration of the second stage is cut approximately in half when the mother is properly trained in the correct posture and good techniques of pushing. Here are some reasons why:

1. You will hold your breath, with a lung full of air, so that the diaphragm (which you have avoided using before this) is deflected downward, exerting pressure on the upper portion of the uterus, the fundus.
2. You will tighten your abdominal muscles, exerting further pressure on the uterus.
3. You will have assumed a posture that curves your back and brings your legs up as high as possible and as far apart as possible to remove any obstruction from in front of your baby's head.
4. You will learn to relax the perineum (the floor of the pelvis) to minimize further any obstructive force.
5. You will follow up that reflex urge by bearing down with all of your might.

So you can see how much additional help you can give the uterus during each expulsion contraction. Remember, this is only *helping* the uterus. Therefore, it would be foolish of you to try to push in between contractions. It would be a waste of energy. You cannot push the baby out without the uterus contracting. Instead, you will use the time in between contractions to rest, because pushing is very hard work.

This pushing will be accompanied in two different settings. First, you will still be in the labor room when the second stage begins. In many hospitals, most of the pushing is done in the labor room so that only a few contractions remain by the time you go to the delivery room.

For the pushing that is done in the labor room, the head of the bed should be elevated to a comfortable position, with two pillows supporting the back and lower shoulders, and when the contraction has begun, the mother's legs will be brought up to her abdomen and held up with her hands underneath her knees. During these contractions, the wife will probably be very grateful for some assistance in supporting her legs. By this time, she may be getting tired, and holding up the weight of the entire legs during each contraction may be difficult for her. The husband can help by standing beside the bed, facing her, and pushing against her knees as they are up in the air; or he can ask a nurse to stand on one side of the bed and support one leg, while he stands on the other side to support the other leg.

For the last part of pushing done in the delivery room, the technique is unchanged, and the posture is essentially the same except that the legs will be supported at the knees by stirrups so that the mother does not have to hold them up. Her hands will be resting underneath the sterile drapes, and when the contraction begins and her doctor instructs her to push, she will take hold of the poles that support the stirrups (or the hand grips that are attached to the table) and pull, to help her raise her shoulders and lean forward on her diaphragm. Therefore, the head of the delivery table does not need to be as high as the head of the bed was in the labor room. You will need to take only the two pillows from the labor bed with you onto the delivery table for support of your head and shoulders when you lie back to relax and rest between contractions.

Before you start to do the practice for pushing, let us pay some attention to the supplemental exercises that will help your actual pushing in labor:

1. *Holding your breath:* Look at the second hand of a clock and see how long you can comfortably hold your breath before having to release it. Of course, no one would expect you to hold your breath for the entire 60 seconds or more that the contraction will last, but it will be to your advantage if you do not have to exchange more air than two more times after the initial intake of air at the start of the contraction. Each time you have to relax your pushing position, exhale, and take in a new breath, the baby's head slips backwards a little. Therefore, you would not make so much progress with each contraction if you had to change air every 5 or 10 seconds as you would if you could hold the air for 20 or 25 seconds before you let go. If you cannot comfortably hold your breath for about 25 seconds, then practice holding your breath and add on a second or two every few days until you can.

2. *Abdominal muscle tone:* In the beginning of your training when you started to learn the body-building exercises, we said that out of those—the pelvic rock—would be helpful in getting some tone back in your abdominal muscles that may have become lax during pregnancy. You will have continued to do the pelvic rock, but now you will add on one other abdominal exercise for improving your musculature:

   Place your hands on your abdomen; inhale a lungful of air; let the same amount of air out; then blow out, using the residual air left in your lungs. You will feel your abdominal muscles tighten up under your hands and get hard. Do this several times a day.

3. *Perineal relaxation:* The area between the vagina and the anus, which constitutes the floor of the pelvis, is called the "perineum," and it is important that these tissues be completely relaxed during the birth of your baby. Perineal relaxation will make for an easier and smoother delivery and will reduce the danger of lacerations.

Sometimes, when she feels the urge to bear down, instead of relaxing the perineum, a mother will respond by tightening up in this area, for fear of having a bowel movement in the bed or as an unconscious effort to resist the sensation of pressure she feels in the rectal area. You can easily see how important it is for you to learn to avoid this tightening. It is exactly counter to all the efforts being made by the contracting uterus and the additional help being given by the rest of your body to move your baby out of the birth canal.

You can learn to relax this part of your body, consciously and deliberately, the same way you have used your neuromuscular control exercises to learn how to relax the other parts of your body when the uterus is contracting. Possibly, in sexual intercourse, you have involuntarily contracted and relaxed these muscles, but before now, there has probably never been a need for you to consciously think, "Now I am going to relax the floor of my pelvis." First, you need to identify where these muscles are and what it feels like when they are relaxed. Then you will learn how to effect this relaxation at will.

You can learn to isolate the area to be relaxed because it is bounded on the back by the anal orifice (opening) and on the front by the urethral orifice, which leads to the bladder, and you can learn to consciously control the area because you already have voluntary control of the sphincters (ring-like muscles) that surround these two openings. In the past, you have deliberately tightened the sphincter around the anus when you did not want to have a bowel movement or tightened the sphincter around the urethra when you did not want to pass urine. Now you will use these sphincters to help you realize the opposite sensation—that of "release."

Sit in a chair with your feet flat on the floor and tightly squeeze the muscles around the anus, as if you were trying to prevent having a bowel movement. Squeeze tighter and tighter, as tight as you can, hold it for a few seconds, and then release. Now do the same thing in front with the muscle around the urethra. Squeeze tightly, as if you were trying to prevent urination or trying to stop in midstream, hold it for a few seconds, and then release. Now try to tighten both at once; think of the anal orifice and tighten; think of the urethral orifice and tighten; and now tighten the entire area between the two, the whole floor of the pelvis. Squeeze as tight as you can, hold it for a few seconds, and release. It is this feeling of *release* that you are pursuing and that you will use during your pushing contractions. The best way to learn it is first to identify and isolate these muscles with your mind, and then to realize the difference in the sensations of "tighten" and "release."

This is a very important exercise! It is important not only during the period when you are pushing in labor, but it is also very beneficial in the postpartum period (after your baby is born) to eliminate, or minimize, the discomfort that frequently accompanies the episiotomy repair—those famous stitches that your friends have told you about.

The advantages realized from doing this exercise bring as many favorable comments on the postpartum reports from my students as any other single exercise they have learned. During the first few days they are in the hospital after the baby is born, the students see the untrained mothers all about them having "trouble with the stitches."

The mere location of the episiotomy probably brings forth more anxiety than if these few stitches were in some other part of the body. For instance, if you had four or five stitches taken in your arm, you would probably not be afraid to make a fist or to bend your elbow. But because these stitches are in such a delicate area, the mothers feel that their stitches must be guarded and protected. This overprotection of the area can increase rather than decrease the stitch discomfort, because much of the "stitch pain" begins as edema (accumulation of fluid) between the stitches. With lack of exercise and poor circulation to the area, this is followed by irritation and inflammation, all of which can be a real nuisance in the postpartum period.

You should start to do this exercise now so that you will be able to relax the perineum during your labor. You should also start to use this exercise early in the postpartum period to keep the area supple, to improve circulation to the area, and to avoid the collection of fluid between the stitches. By doing so, you can help to avoid stitch discomfort as well as the nuisance of treatments with heat lamps, anesthetic sprays, etc., that go along with it.

Many times, patients who have faithfully done this exercise will comment on the ease with which they passed their urine after their babies were born, at the same time their postpartum roommates are having difficulty with urination or bowel movements, sometimes to the point of having to be catheterized or requiring laxatives.

It is a simple little exercise that is easy to do, but one that can be very important to you during labor, postpartum period, and possibly even in later years. Keep it up!

Now, let us go back to the actual exercise for pushing in labor. It may have seemed like an awful lot to learn when we first listed all the parts of your body that are involved in pushing, but it is really not so hard to remember if you will start with your usual deep, cleansing breath and then ''think your way'' downward from your head to your feet, adding on, one by one, the other parts of the body as you go:

1. Deep, cleansing breaths: Take two inhalations-exhalations, and with the third inhalation, hold your breath. These two breaths will allow time for the uterine contraction to build up to the point where your pushing efforts will be most meaningful.
2. Bend your head so that your chin comes down toward your chest.
3. Round your shoulders so that you are ''leaning'' on your diaphragm with your lungs full of air.
4. Put your hands underneath your bent knees and bring your legs up as high as you can, and as far apart as you can, holding your elbows slightly out in the air, rather than in close to your sides.
5. Tighten your abdominal muscles.
6. Release your perineal muscles.

7. Bear down, keeping in mind that you are pushing your baby forward toward the vaginal opening.
8. Maintain this pushing effort as long as you can comfortably hold your breath, then release, exhale, take in another breath, and start all over again.
9. Continue in this fashion until the end of the contraction and then take two or three deep, cleansing breaths, and allow yourself to relax all over so that you can rest until the next contraction begins. This rest period, although brief, is very important, because during the contraction, you will be working very hard.

You should get into this position every day and go through the steps outlined above. If you are afraid that you might rupture membranes when practicing, or if your doctor advises against it, you do not have to bear down as hard as you will in actual labor (since daily conditioning is not important in bearing down), but you do need to practice the pushing posture and procedures so that (a) you will not be embarrassed or ill at ease to assume this posture when your doctor tells you it's time to push, and (b) so that in labor, you will be able to remember all the parts of your body to use.

To Stop Pushing

Earlier, I indicated that the work you do in the second stage is "more brawn than brain." There is, however, one instance while you are pushing on the delivery table that requires a great deal of mental effort. That is when you are pushing as hard as you can, bearing down with all your might, and your doctor, right in the middle of a contraction, tells you to stop pushing. He does this in order to regulate the speed of the delivery and make it a smooth, even procedure. When your doctor gives this instruction to stop pushing, you should let go of the stirrup poles you are holding on to, lie back on your pillows, switch immediately to your panting or pant-blow breathing as you relax your body and let the uterus finish the job. Following this instruction requires some effort, but it is a very welcome sound, because the next instruction from your doctor will probably be the nicest thing you have ever heard him say: "Now take a look at your new baby."

Coach

The coach shares with the laboring woman the joining of tasks. The helper is like the lookout on a yacht sailing at night, watching for the coastline and helping to steer her through. Giving support in labor requires compassion, skill, patience, and understanding. An awareness of what the laboring woman is thinking and feeling at each moment, and complete commitment to the task. It can be hard, exhausting work. The excitement, the deep satisfaction, and the joy when a child is born is shared by the coach.

THE THIRD STAGE

Your doctor will again ask you to bear down to deliver the placenta after it separates from the uterus. While he repairs the episiotomy under anesthetics any discomfort may be helped by relaxing with the breathing techniques used during the first stage of labor and by observing your beautiful new infant.

9
THE NEWBORN

THE DELIVERY ROOM

The birth of your baby will be one of the most exhilarating and rewarding experiences you have ever had. If you are awake during the event itself, you will notice a very funny sequence of events.

Until the moment of birth itself, all eyes will be focused on you in anticipation. After the birth, you will be able to relax for the first time in quite a few hours, while the doctor and nurses scurry about to accommodate the new citizen of the world.

After the baby is born and lets out its first cry, it is placed on sterile sheets for you to look at while the umbilical cord is clamped and cut. The nose and mouth will be cleared to facilitate breathing. A bracelet will be put on the baby for identification. His footprint, with your fingerprint, will be placed on a card to register the event officially. Some doctors will place the baby on your abdomen at first.

While you are delivering the placenta and having the episiotomy repaired, the baby will be cleaned up, and the umbilical cord may be further shortened and clamped. An injection of vitamin K may also be given to him. The nurses will remove the cheesy white material called "vernix caseosa," which protected his skin during gestation. Large babies and postmature babies have very little of this coating on their skin at birth. The nurses may also place in the baby's eyes a 1 percent solution of silver nitrate to prevent the effect of maternal gonorrhea on the newborn's eyes. Some hospitals use penicillin or tetracycline for this purpose.

You may hear the nurses mentioning numbers. They probably refer to the Apgar score. At birth, a general evaluation system is used by most institutions to score the physical condition of the infant for purposes of prognosis and treatment. The system is named after Dr. Virginia Apgar, an anesthesiologist who, in the 1950's, was active in newborn medicine and obstetrical anesthesia.

The infant is evaluated on the basis of five signs and given a point score of 0 to 2 for each of these five signs. A 10 would be the highest score. As seen on the following chart, the infants can be graded from 0 to 10.

Follow-up studies over the past 15 years have shown that infants with Apgar scores of less than 4 have a higher incidence of neurological problems and defects over the years.

APGAR SCORING CHART

Sign	0	1	2
Heart Rate	Absent	Slow (below 100)	Over 100
Respiratory Effort	Absent	Weak cry	Good strong cry
Muscle Tone	Limp	Some flexion of extremities	Well flexed
Reflex Response — Response to catheter in nostril (tested after oropharynx is clear)	No	Grimace	Cough or sneeze
Foot slap	No	Grimace	Cry and withdrawal of foot

Color	Blue pale		Body pink; extremities blue	Completely pink

Apgar Score	= 7–10	=	Good infant
	4–6	=	Moderately depressed infant
	3 or below =		Severely depressed infant

THE NURSERY

When all of this is finished, and after you have held or breast-fed your baby, the baby is taken to the nursery, where most of its needs will be met for the next few days. Nurses will check its bowel movements, which are brownish-green for the first few days after birth. In this form, the stool is called "meconium." They will check to make certain the baby is voiding feces and urine. Failure to do so may indicate some congenital problem in need of correction. They will check for a jaundice which occurs in about a third of all newborns. This is caused by an immaturity of the baby's liver, with a resulting increase in bile pigment.

The nurses will change and bathe the baby and help you with feeding and learning about being a mother.

A pediatrician or general practitioner should at this point take over the care of the infant. Most hospitals give the baby to the mother for feedings, whether the baby is breast- or bottle-fed. All babies lose weight immediately after birth. Most are too sleepy to eat the first few days. But when they are ready, they will let you know. No baby starves quietly.

ROOMING-IN

In some hospitals, babies can stay in the rooms with their mothers. This arrangement is called "rooming-in." There are pros and cons.

Proponents say it is good for several reasons. Since the baby is in the room with the mother to be fed on demand, rooming-in promotes lactation for breast-feeding. They say the mother's attention will be focused on baby care immediately, reducing her worry about what will happen at home. Then, once she gets home, caring for the baby won't seem so strange to her. She will also learn the demands of most newborns are not so great—they sleep about 20 out of 24 hours a day. Fathers also can spend more time with their newborns when they room-in.

Opponents do not agree. They say rooming-in is not necessary, especially for a mother who does not feel well after delivery. They feel that four or five days are not going to make that much difference in learning to be a mother, since the mother and baby have the rest of their lives to become acquainted in the comfort of their home. Some opponents are against the idea of paying for the high cost of postpartum care and then doing all the work themselves.

FEEDING

The decision to breast-feed or bottle-feed is a mother's personal preference. Just as many mothers were attracted to general anesthesia for delivery when it became widely used in the 1940's, so were many mothers attracted to bottle-feeding when prepared formulas became more widely available, reducing the need to make formula. Bottle-feeding today can be as easy as screwing a sterilized nipple onto a bottle of prepared formula that requires no refrigeration until it is opened. But the pendulum of maternal and medical preferences seems to be swinging back to "the more natural" way of child caring, meaning an increasing number of nursing mothers.

Breast milk has special properties that make it superior to even the most carefully made home or commercial preparations. It not only provides substances (antibodies) that protect against common childhood illnesses, such as colds and respiratory disease, but also helps produce a protective environment against infection in the intestinal tract. It contains the complete range of nutrients necessary to the young infant and is easier to digest than substitutes. Breast-feeding costs less (it's free!) than feeding with substitutes. While nursing eliminates formula and bottle preparation, it requires a more careful diet and a little more privacy at mealtime, unless you feel natural enough with the process to nurse the baby in public. As you see, this is no either/or proposition. Women who have generally busy schedules or who return to work when the baby is very young, nurse for some meals and bottle-feed for others. The baby's demand will determine the supply of breast milk.

Besides being the best form of nutrition for the infant, breast-feeding may be an important means of spacing births and preventing pregnancy, especially in religious groups who cannot use artificial methods of contraception.

For those who do decide to nurse, some background will be useful.

Throughout pregnancy, the breasts are sensitive to the hormonal changes in the body. Very early, the breast becomes enlarged, and the nipples grow larger and darker in color. By the end of the third month, a premilk, called "colostrum," is formed and may ooze from the nipples throughout pregnancy. The amount of colostrum increases just after delivery. Until the milk comes in, the baby will drink colostrum.

When the milk does come in, your breasts may be painful and engorged. For up to ten days, milk and colostrum are secreted. The milk does not become a stable, nutritious compound until about a month following delivery. Thereafter, the supply of milk is determined by the amount of sucking by the baby, which is why it is suggested that you start the baby on both breasts at each feeding to get the milk to flow.

Breast milk as a food contains protein, carbohydrates, and fat in sufficient quantities to make it a complete food. Except for vitamins B and D, and iron, breast milk contains all the vitamins a growing baby needs. These other substances will probably be prescribed as a supplement by the pediatrician.

There are several factors which will determine how satisfying nursing will be for the baby. Besides the baby's demand, the amount of milk available also depends on a satisfactory schedule, an adequate diet for the mother including a good deal of liquids, an emotionally relaxing environment, general good health, and good care of the breasts to prevent cracking. This last condition can be prevented by using a good cream on the breasts and by letting them dry off after a feeding. A breast shield can also be used to protect tender nipples. Breasts should be supported by a firm brassiere for comfort and to eliminate sagging after you stop nursing. See the suggestions for successful breast-feeding at the end of this chapter.

THE PEDIATRICIAN

At the hospital, your baby will be checked thoroughly by a staff pediatrician. You can, however, have the pediatrician of your choice come to the hospital and check your baby in most instances. Many mothers find this practice tremendously helpful. The doctor will look at the baby from stem to stern and alert the mother to little birthmarks and rashes which might frighten her when she discovers them at home. Since most mothers are lying in high, narrow beds when the baby is given to them for feeding, they never unwrap the baby until they get him home.

The doctor will also give feeding instructions and will answer any questions you may have. He will also tell you certain things to look for—girl babies, for example, often have a slightly bloody vaginal discharge soon after birth. A mother seeing this in a week-old baby, without expecting it, could be quite upset.

The doctor will also set up an office appointment for you to bring the baby in for a weigh-in, checkup and immunization after his first month and every month thereafter until the baby is about eight months old, when visits become less frequent.

CARE AT HOME

Some women are afraid they will have a baby who cries insistently and inconsolably. Actually, newborn babies usually cry for only a few reasons: they are hungry or thirsty, too cold or too hot, or sleepy. Where the adult human is ruled by his brain, the infant is ruled by the stomach. Most chronically unhappy babies have some kind of digestive disturbance, and most of these have some medical remedy. Often, the baby just needs more to eat or may need solid foods. Some doctors are prescribing cereal as early as the second or third week of life. Colic, the early indigestion, is often caused by intolerance to cow's milk. Breast milk or goat's milk is often used as a substitute.

It has been pretty well established that a newborn does not have the cerebral capacity to be spoiled. Being spoiled requires some memory development, which he could not have as yet. The current thinking among child psychologists is to view crying as a physical need which should be tended to. The thinking here is that by answering the need, you teach the child patience by showing him that the world is a friendly place which takes care of him.

Newborns want to be warm and snug as they were inside Mama. This is why a baby might cry when its clothes are taken off. It is also the reason that even in summer babies are usually wrapped snugly in little cotton flannel receiving blankets until they get used to being on the outside.

The most common questions which arise concerning newborn care are among the following:

1. *Scheduling*—In past generations, a good deal of effort went into putting the baby on a regular schedule. Mothers sat waiting for the minute hand to hit the hour before they fed a baby who had been crying for a half-hour. Or they woke up a perfectly contented sleeping baby because it was "his time to eat." But because he was not really hungry, he would not really eat, meaning he probably would awaken before his next scheduled feeding, demanding food.

   Modern mothers are much more relaxed and much more likely to feed the baby when it says it is hungry. Actually, most mothers find that, if left to regulate themselves, most babies want to eat about every four hours. Some eat more often, some less often. Larger babies who have bigger stomachs that can accommodate more food will probably eat less frequently. As a rule of thumb, a baby who eats everything at every meal is probably not getting enough to eat. Most of the babycare books have tables to use as informal guides to the amount a child should be eating, according to its size.

2. *Sleeping*—A newborn baby usually sleeps more than it is awake. For most mothers, this is a welcome opportunity to rest. Mothers who are eager to interact with their baby find it difficult to feed, clothe, bathe, cuddle, and then just put down this new lethargic family member. Eventually, however, the sleeping beauty does awaken, and you may then hope for the return of the angelic little sleeping child whom you wished would wake up.

3. *Care of the cord*—There will be a scab on the baby's belly where the umbilical cord attached him to the mother. About ten days following birth, this drying remnant of a cord will fall off, leaving in its place the navel or "belly button." Until this happens, however, the cord should be cleaned off daily with an alcohol pad. If possible, the baby's diaper should not cover the cord. You should refrain from bathing the baby in a tub until the cord falls off.

4. *Bathing the baby*—For the first few days, the baby should be given sponge baths. If possible, only a little part of the baby should be exposed and washed at a time, so he remains comfortable and warm. Most hospitals provide instructions for bathing the baby in prenatal classes or in mothers' classes after birth.

5. *Fresh air*—Fresh air is usually recommended for new babies, weather permitting. In summer, fresh air is no problem. When you should take the baby out in winter is another matter. Your doctor will give you specific instructions, usually based on your baby's size. There is a tremendous tendency for new mothers to overdress babies when they take them out. Remember—they require no more clothing in any weather than you do.

6. *Circumcision*—Removal of the foreskin of the newborn male's penis has been quite common, even in non-Jewish families. Its benefits, however, are still debated. It is best to discuss this with your physician. It is usually performed before seven days and appears quite harmless and simple to do.

SUGGESTIONS FOR SUCCESSFUL BREAST-FEEDING

Here are some suggestions which have proved helpful to many mothers in continuing to breast-feed after they have left the hospital. Your doctor may feel that some points should be modified for you or your baby. Remember that he is seeing your individual baby and making recommendations accordingly. He will be glad to explain if you tell him you would like to understand the reasons for his recommendations.

1. The bowel movements of the breast-fed baby are typically soft, even liquid in consistency, yellowish-brown or greenish-brown in color, and may have curds or mucus present. They may occur as seldom as once every other day or occasionally once in three days, but most often are present at every feeding. Thus, what would certainly be called diarrhea in an adult or formula-fed infant is the normal bowel movement of the breast-fed baby. If anything else seems to indicate illness, your baby should be checked by a doctor.

2. The breast-fed baby typically demands and needs to eat about every three hours when he first leaves the hospital. Formula-fed infants typically eat less frequently at first. The breast-fed baby may also gain at a slower rate than the formula-fed baby, but this is fine so long as the gain is sufficient and the baby is otherwise well. Since some babies are not so efficient at making their needs known as others, it is a good idea to try to nurse your baby more often than demanded during the first month, if the baby does not demand at least six feedings a day. At the time of the baby's one-month-old checkup, it is a good idea to check with the doctor if you wish to try to feed less often.

3. If at any time you or your doctor feel that your supply of breast milk is not fully meeting the baby's needs, you can usually build it up to the required level by nursing as often as possible for 48 hours (as often as every two hours during the day and every three at night) while trying to rest and take fluids. Most babies have times when they suddenly seem hungry, but this need not mean your supply has dwindled—the baby may suddenly need more because he is growing in spurts. If you nurse more often for a few days, you will probably find that baby returns to his former schedule and seems happy with it again, because he is now getting more milk at each nursing.

4. If you really want to nurse your baby, it is likely to work best if you do not leave a nighttime bottle during the first month. Sometimes, the nighttime bottle does work out, but often the mother finds that her supply is scanty by the time the baby is a few weeks old. If you

do have help at home, it is best used for housekeeping, shopping, preparation of meals, and perhaps some care of the baby between feedings, rather than for feedings themselves. Once the baby is about a month old, however, leaving a bottle for one to three feedings per week will not interfere with continued breast-feeding. After several months, even a daily bottle will not interfere.

5. When you first get home, it is advisable to continue to limit the time on each breast at each feeding to 10 to 12 minutes (not counting time when the baby dozes). Prolonged feedings may lead to soreness, while frequent, short feedings should not. Remember that the baby takes the major portion of the milk present in the breast in about 5 to 7 minutes of sucking time. After you are sure that you will still be comfortable, there is no harm in letting the baby nurse longer at some or all feedings if you and baby both wish to. However, this is not necessary for the baby's nutrition. If baby wants additional sucking time, this is because many babies have a need to suck that is greater than what is required for getting food. Some mothers supply this need by additional time on the breast, some by using pacifiers or empty bottles with blind nipples, and some by giving boiled water between feedings. Water is not needed, however, by the healthy breast-fed baby, except sometimes in very hot weather or if the temperature of your home is high.

6. Your doctor or clinic will make recommendations to you as to when to introduce the baby to juice and to solid foods. The breast milk does contain everything the baby needs for nutrition except for some vitamins and iron. A vitamin supplement will probably be prescribed for your baby. The healthy infant does not need iron until 4 to 6 months. Therefore, solid foods are not nutritionally needed by most breast-fed babies for quite a while. Solid foods may be suggested earlier, but often your doctor will be willing to have you wait if you tell him you wish to do so. The baby who has started solids is naturally less eager to nurse and may slacken his nursing enough to lower his

mother's supply even below what he still needs. Also, the younger the baby, the greater the chance that introduction of a food other than breast milk will elicit an allergic response. The later you start solids, the less the likelihood that they will interfere with adequate milk supply.

7. Remember that baby may cry for many reasons besides hunger. Some of the things worth trying in order to soothe the crying baby are swaddling (wrapping baby with arms at his sides in a light blanket), burping, changing diapers, adding or removing a layer of clothing or of blanketing in case baby is uncomfortably cool or warm, rocking, and offering pacifiers. The "test" of trying to determine whether the baby is hungry by offering a bottle is inadvisable, since many breast-fed babies will drink from a bottle even when their weight before and after nursing shows they have been well fed. In general, offering a bottle because of possible hunger only causes the baby to wait longer before nursing again, and this does decrease the mother's supply.

8. It is perfectly normal for your breasts to lose their initial hardness and gradually to return to normal size even while you continue breast-feeding. This does not mean you are losing your milk—in about six months, you should be back to your nonpregnant size even if the baby is fed only from the breast and, of course, is taking much more milk than at six days, when you were probably quite big.

9. You may not menstruate for quite a while if you continue to breast-feed. This is normal and no cause for concern. When your periods do resume, they may be irregular for a while, and the baby may appear to be fussy for a day or two. Your milk is just as good at this time, however, and baby should continue to be breast-fed. It is possible to ovulate while you are breast-feeding even if you have not yet menstruated since the baby was born, so that you can become pregnant again without ever menstruating. Although birth-control pills are inadvisable while breast-feeding, since they do tend to dry up the milk, your doctor or

clinic can suggest other means of family planning if you wish. If you should become pregnant, it is usually felt that you should wean the baby who is breast-feeding, but that this be done gradually rather than suddenly.

10. The best time to wean the baby is when you want to. If you wish to breast-feed for a relatively short time and then stop, most authorities feel it is better to stop than to continue reluctantly. However, if you wish to continue for a relatively long time, there is no time at which your milk becomes a poor food for your baby. At about six months, though, it is no longer adequate as the *only* food. Our hope is not that you will breast-feed for any specified length of time, but that you will stop because you are ready and wish to, rather than because of poor information or lack of support. Weaning should be done gradually for your own comfort and the easiest transition for the baby. This means that you substitute the bottle (or cup, with an older baby) for the breast at one feeding a day for several days, until you find you no longer feel full at that feeding, then eliminate a second breast-feeding for a few days, etc.

11. Mothers often ask if it is all right to breast-feed the baby when they themselves are ill. Unless the mother must take medication which would harm the baby by passing through the milk, or unless the mother has an illness which does not permit her to have contact with the baby, regardless of how she feels, it is perfectly all right, providing that her doctor does not order otherwise. For example, you do not protect a breast-fed baby from catching your cold by giving a bottle instead of the breast, since the baby is equally exposed to your germs while being bottle-fed. Medications taken by the mother should be checked with the baby's doctor, however, since you want to be very careful about what substances reach the baby through the milk. Antihistamines temporarily decrease your milk supply and should be avoided unless essential to your health.

12. You may hear many do's and don't'ss of diet while breast-feeding, most of which you can ignore. In general, you can eat what you wish, as far as your milk and the

baby's health are concerned, but a good diet is naturally preferable to a poor one for your own health, just as at any other time. It is advisable to make sure that you get enough calcium by drinking several glasses of milk a day or substituting cheeses, ice cream, puddings, and other foods containing milk (skim milk is just as good as whole milk in providing calcium). Since you do not need to eat fatty foods and will need about 1,000 calories more a day than if you were not breast-feeding, you certainly need not gain weight or remain heavy in order to breast-feed. In fact, this is a good time for the really overweight woman to lose some weight while the underweight woman should attempt to eat more for her own sake during the nursing period. So few babies react with any appearance of digestive upset to any one food that we suggest eating as you wish and then eliminating any food that you suspect bothers your baby if baby seems upset several times after you have eaten it. There is no particular food or beverage that helps to make milk or improve its quality and which you therefore should eat or drink. It is important to drink enough fluids (water is as good for this purpose as any other beverage), since lack of fluids can decrease your milk supply, but once you are drinking enough, extra fluids won't make more milk. Drink whenever you are thirsty and try to drink something at each nursing, but you need not drink to the point of discomfort. Alcoholic beverages and coffee and tea will not affect the milk in a manner harmful to the baby unless taken in large quantities.

13. You may hear that a woman must be calm and relaxed in order to breast-feed successfully. The truth is that anxiety, tension, and fatigue do not lessen the mother's supply of milk, but they may make it difficult for her to release or let down milk that is present in her breasts. Therefore, it is desirable to make an effort to arrange for circumstances that will permit you to be as calm and comfortable as possible shortly before and during each nursing. It will perhaps help your confidence and ability to release your milk if you try to remember that

many busy, active, not especially relaxed women have successfully breast-fed their children.

14. The biggest question in the minds of most women who are breast-feeding is whether the baby is getting enough milk. It is hard for many women to believe that they can produce enough milk for their babies, when they hear so much about breast-feeding being difficult for modern women, and they may envy the ability of the woman who bottle-feeds to count the ounces that the baby takes. Unfortunately, weighing the baby often, and especially before and after feeding, creates a really interfering state of worry in most mothers and is advisable only for the small minority of cases where a doctor feels the baby has not been gaining well enough and the mother wishes to see if more frequent feedings improve matters enough in the time the doctor feels can be allowed for this.

MANUAL EXPRESSION OF BREAST MILK
(Removing Breast Milk with Your Hands)

I. When do you use manual expression?
  1. To stimulate and increase your supply of milk.
  2. To relieve a full, uncomfortable breast.
  3. To maintain your supply of milk if the baby is temporarily unable to feed at the breast.
  4. To give the infant breast milk in a relief bottle.
II. What equipment do you need?
  1. If the milk is not going to be given to the baby, it can be expressed directly into the sink or any available container and then discarded.
  2. Breast milk is sterile as it leaves the breast. No further sterilization is necessary.
III. How can you make manual expression work?
  1. Wash your hands.
  2. Expose the breast.
  3. Gently wash your breasts with a soft cloth and plain water. Pat dry with a soft towel.
  4. Assume a comfortable position.

BREAST-FEEDING SCHEDULE

	2:00 a.m.	6:00 a.m.	10:00 a.m.	2:00 p.m.	6:00 p.m.	10:00 p.m.
FIRST DAY 2–3 minutes on each breast	Glucose water in nursery	To mother	To mother	To mother	To mother	To mother
		Glucose water after feeding	Glucose water after feeding	Glucose water after feeding	Glucose water after feeding	Glucose water after feeding
SECOND DAY 3–5 minutes on each breast	Glucose water in nursery	Same as above	Same as above	Same as above	Same as above	Same as above
THIRD DAY 5–7 minutes on each breast	Glucose water in nursey	Same as above	Same as above	Same as above	Same as above	Same as above
FOURTH DAY 10 minutes on each breast	To mother	To mother	To mother	To mother	To mother	To mother
	Weighed before and after feeding*	No water after feeding	No water after feeding	No water after feeding	No water after feeding	No water after feeding
FIFTH DAY and thereafter	Repeat as for the FOURTH DAY, except weighing of infant.					

*The infant is weighed before and after a feeding to estimate the fluid intake.
1. At each feeding, begin with the breast from which the baby nursed last.
2. Nipple shields are used only when ordered by your doctor.

5. Place a towel or cloth under the breast to protect your clothing if the milk should drip.

6. Hold the pitcher or container beneath the nipple. The container should be sterile if the milk is to be given to the infant.

7. Grasp the breast gently just back of the aureola (brown part of the breast) with the ball of the thumb on the upper surface of the breast and the forefinger beneath the lower surface.

8. Press the thumb and forefinger together gently, but firmly, squeezing that part of the breast between them.

9. With a forward pull and downward pressure, the milk is forced out in a stream without your fingers touching the nipple.

10
POSTPARTUM CARE

There is probably no more neglected stage of childbirth for the mother than the period immediately following the birth of the baby. So much energy and interest are directed to the event itself that often there is less preparation for the period following delivery.

For one thing, you will be tired. Labor requires an expenditure of energy equal to that needed for a 12-mile hike, and while this is more than compensated for by the exhilaration of birth itself, the postpartum period can be a little anticlimactic. Your doctor, who paid very close attention to you those last few weeks, relaxes more about your condition once he is certain you are fine. The stitches which closed the episiotomy will hurt. Most women do not anticipate or are not prepared for the pain that may be present in the episiotomy. This is temporary (4 to 5 days usually) and can be greatly alleviated by analgesics, local preparations, and sitz baths. Pain is not necessarily over once the baby is delivered.

Hemorrhoids can also develop after birth, especially after prolonged pushing in the second stage of labor. These painful engorged veins about the rectal area are also temporary and can be relieved by various medications.

Uterine cramps are bothersome after delivery, especially when breast feeding. Uterine cramps usually last for less than a week and are worse in multiparas. Analgesics are useful in this regard. Uterine cramps are a manifestation of the body getting back to its normal state.

A few days following delivery, you may become very depressed for no apparent reason. This postpartum depression, or "baby blues," is not clearly understood, but is rather common and should be no cause for concern.

The discomforts of the episiotomy, hemorrhoids, or uterine cramps may add to your "blues." But remember, these are temporary discomforts which can be greatly alleviated by medications. It won't be long before you are feeling great and strolling with your new infant in the park for all to admire.

Basically, you must remember to prepare for the period following birth as actively as you prepared for birth itself. This may include hiring a nurse or inviting a family member to come help with cleaning, cooking, caring for other children, or showing you how to take care of the baby when you come home from the hospital.

GENERAL INSTRUCTIONS

After delivery, you will be taken to your room to rest. The baby may not be brought to you for the first 8 to 12 hours to allow you both time to get acclimated. Recently, many hospitals have instituted programs allowing the newborn infant to be with the parents for a while after birth. This seems to improve bonding between parents and child.

You will be encouraged to urinate so that a tube will not have to be passed into the bladder to help you void. This procedure, called "catheterization," is often required when prolonged labor has weakened the bladder muscles.

You will probably be given pain relievers for the stitches and heat-lamp treatments or sitz baths for the episiotomy and hemorrhoids. A cream will be supplied to put on the stitches to keep them moist. When they dry out, they have a tendency to pull. The nurses will show you how to change your sanitary pads and clean off after you go to the bathroom, to prevent infected stitches.

You should move your bowels within four days following delivery. If you do not, a mild laxative or a gentle enema or suppositories are often required. They will be welcomed.

A non-nursing mother requires no special breast care except a good support bra. Non-nursing mothers are sometimes given pills to prevent lactation. Mothers who have breast engorgement can use ice packs and pain relievers, and restrict fluid intake for about two days, allowing the problem to solve itself. Nursing mothers suffering from engorgement can squeeze some of the fluid out, either by hand or by using the hospital's breast pump. If you are Rh negative and your baby is Rh positive you should receive your immunization with Rh immunoglobin within 72 hours after delivery. (See Chapter 11.)

Upon returning home, you should rest for the first few weeks, resuming normal activity slowly, as tolerance permits. Socializing should be kept to a minimum. You will be tired enough receiving family and friends who come to see the baby.

You should bathe daily. Baths will help the episiotomy and primping a little will make you feel better.

Begin exercising slowly. Walking the baby is probably as much as you will need to do for a little while. Many women like to do exercises to firm up stomach muscles. Ask your doctor when you can start these.

You should refrain from intercourse for the first six weeks following delivery to give your body a chance to return to normal, to allow the stitches to heal and to avoid the possibility of infection. Upon resumption of sexual relations, you may experience some discomfort for a while. Pain of some sort is common. With patience, relaxation, lubricants if necessary, and tender loving care, this too will soon end, and sexual relations will be normal again.

If the vagina feels relaxed and open upon resuming sexual activity, the so-called Kegel exercises can help. These exercises consist of voluntarily squeezing the muscles of the anal, vaginal, and urethral areas (as outlined in Chapter 8 under "Perineal Relaxation"). As the frequency of these voluntary contractions increase, this isometric exercise will increase vaginal tone.

While pregnancy and postpartum care are states of health and not illness, a little conservative management does not hurt. Rest will determine the milk production in a nursing mother and will, therefore, determine how satisfied the baby's needs are. Try to take a nap each day. You may drive after one or two weeks.

PHYSICAL CHANGES AND EXERCISES

While everything appears to return to normal very quickly, physical changes occur in the body for a long time following delivery.

The organs of reproduction begin returning to their pre-pregnant state almost immediately in a process known as "involution." The uterus slowly shrinks in size, going from one and one-half pounds the first week following delivery to its normal weight of two ounces.

The vagina and external genitalia, which stretched tremendously for delivery, gradually regain their muscle tone over an eight-week period. The vaginal opening also becomes smaller as muscles firm up.

The uterus continues to shed the lining it used to support birth. This discharge is called "lochia." Lochia is bloody at first and then becomes white in color and creamy in consistency. It has a characteristic odor, which offends some women. Lochia usually stops three to six weeks following delivery.

The time of the return of menstruation and ovulation will depend on whether or not you are nursing. Menstruation returns in the first three months following delivery for 90 percent of non-nursing mothers. The hormonal changes caused by lactation generally delay the return of menstruation, although most nursing women will have a period long before nursing is finished.

The delay of ovarian function in nursing has led many women to think that nursing is a good method of contraception. It is not.

Many women find that muscular tone in the abdomen returns very slowly. The rate at which this occurs is determined by several factors, including the individual mother's muscle constitution and the amount of stretching the abdomen has undergone. There are exercises to remedy this, and they are outlined below.

Postpartum Exercises
1st Week:
1. Leg Raising—Lie flat. Raise your legs alternately six inches, keeping them straight, 4 or 5 times.
2. Tightening Abdominal Muscles—Lie on your back. Con-

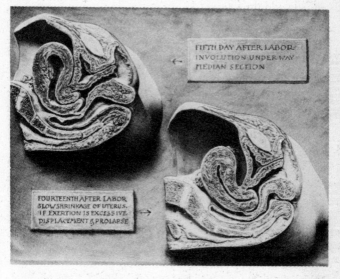

FIFTH DAY AFTER LABOR
INVOLUTION UNDER WAY
MEDIAN SECTION

FOURTEENTH AFTER LABOR
SLOW SHRINKAGE OF UTERUS.
IF EXERTION IS EXCESSIVE
DISPLACEMENT & PROLAPSE

The uterus shrinks slowly in size. Within six weeks after delivery it again occupies its normal position in the pelvis. *Courtesy Maternity Center Association, New York City.*

tract abdominal muscles, then arch your back and push your seat against the floor, then push your back against the floor and raise your pelvic area, 4 to 5 times.

2nd Week:
Increase the number of times you do the above exercises and add the following:
Pelvic Twist—Lying flat on your back, bring knees to chest, arms out straight to sides, keep shoulders flat and twist pelvic area so that left knee touches the floor. Rest, then do a right pelvic twist. Work up slowly to ten twists.

3rd Week:
In addition to the above, you can start sit-ups. With knees bent, flat on your back, and arms in front, raise yourself slowly at the waist. It will help if your toes are placed under a couch or ledge for countertraction. This exercise will be difficult at first, but in the long run, it will get your abdominal muscles back into shape. Work up slowly to 10 to 20 per day.

4th to 6th week:
Walking, jogging, tennis, swimming, etc., can be restarted and prepregnancy levels slowly attained again.

The Six-Week Checkup

Six weeks after delivery is the customary time to see your doctor for a checkup. Your doctor will weigh you, check your breasts, do a pelvic exam and a Pap smear. Any questions about sexual hygiene, contraception, and minor physical concerns should be asked.

At this time, you can be refitted for a diaphragm, an IUD (intrauterine device) can be inserted, or you can be started on birth control pills if you are not breast-feeding. The go-ahead for sexual relations is usually given at this time.

You should continue to see your doctor on a regular basis twice a year if you are taking birth control pills, once per year otherwise for a general checkup.

ON BECOMING A PARENT

After waiting nine long months, you suddenly are a parent. Recent studies have shown that early and close contact between you and your infant leads to a special attachment called "bonding." This bonding process, whereby parents and their baby become closely attached to each other through touching, eye contact, and face to face relationship will help you be relaxed about handling and caring for a tiny baby. This process is the first step toward becoming a closely knit family. It will also help your newborn begin to develop emotionally and socially.

Take every opportunity to become acquainted with your new baby as soon as possible after birth. Every time you pick up your baby, you increase the feeling of belonging to each other. Hold your baby close, talk, sing, cuddle, look into his or her eyes. Even the newborn can detect a warm, friendly presence and respond in many ways.

By the close contact with your baby in the hospital, you will get to know a great deal about each other. At home, your mutual interests will grow stronger every day, although your baby will be mostly self-centered during the first months. Babies crying usually means discomfort or hunger. There are times, however, when babies cry even though there are no obvious reasons. If you have checked your baby and found nothing wrong, crying will not necessarily harm your baby. He may simply want your attention. Don't hesitate, however, to show your love by holding, patting, and kissing. I believe that parents don't spoil babies by loving them. However, if your baby frequently cries for long periods of time, your doctor can best decide whether or not the crying is significant. As time goes by, your infant will become more familiar with the sound of your voice. Talk to your baby while you bathe, diaper, play, and feed him or her. Your baby will eventually respond to the rhythm and tone of your voice with smiles, sounds, and gestures long before he knows what you are saying. Communication systems will gradually develop. They are special for you, and your baby will make you aware of likes and dislikes in a private way.

Your baby's daily life will consist of many feedings, naps,

baths, and eventually daytime walks. Establishing a predictable daily routine makes the baby feel more secure and more relaxed. It may even help develop memory skills. An orderly routine will also help you to be more organized and efficient in baby care. As the weeks go by, your baby will grow and learn. However, no two babies are exactly alike, and your baby won't develop according to a precise schedule in a book. The individual pace is what makes your baby unique. It allows him or her to develop a personality and achieve new accomplishments. Development, however, takes time. Encourage your baby but do not push.

Both physical and emotional growth occur together. In addition to rapid growth in weight and length, development will occur in coordination of the muscles, recognition of objects and people, and increasing ability to perform little tasks. Don't forget that your baby's an individual who is different from any other baby. Your doctor will evaluate your baby's physical and emotional progress during periodic checks.

Being a Father

A good opportunity for baby and father to be alone together is during night feedings. If the baby is not being breast-fed or if supplemental bottles are occasionally used, this private time together while the rest of the family is asleep helps a father and baby form a special closeness. I still remember my night feedings of my daughters while everyone else was asleep. A close relationship with the new baby starts during the pregnancy, and continues in the hospital and at home. Many fathers feel a little insecure about handling a baby because of little experience in doing so, but your baby won't mind if you are awkward. Giving love is much more important than changing a diaper expertly or holding a baby just right.

Since the advent of the prepared childbirth classes and Lamaze deliveries, fathers have become a very vital part of the birth process. This should continue at home.

Being a Mother

Delivery is a strenuous physical experience. Your body will need rest. In order to get that rest, you cannot permit the baby to demand your attention every minute. Child-rearing should not become exhausting. Other members of the family and the father should share in child care and household tasks. This will enable you to overcome your tiredness, rest and feel better about yourself and your baby.

Becoming a mother should not interfere with your being a person in your own right. All of your normal activities should resume approximately 4 to 6 weeks after delivery. You should begin to concentrate on looking and feeling your best. Some depression or blueness is common during the first few months. You may miss your job or your freedom. The demands of continued baby care may be exhausting. It's best at these times to have someone else take care of the baby so you can get out, visit a friend, have dinner, go to the movies, or do whatever else you enjoy. Your baby will be there when you return, and you will miss it and feel more like being with him or her than ever before.

Many professional women will get back to work 6 to 8 weeks after delivery. Ambivalent feelings about leaving the baby can be present. I believe that in the long run, if you are happy and satisfied parents, your baby and children will reflect this.

There are many mixed emotions about becoming a parent, especially if depression occurs. Parents may even find themselves resenting the baby and feeling guilty, or have fears about their ability to become a parent. These feelings are not unusual. Most people have them at some time after the baby comes. If you do your best, you probably will be better parents than you think you are. If you try to be perfect, you certainly will fall short.

Remember, find time for yourself. Babies do not have the right to dominate their parents' personal lives. It is important to you as an individual to keep those interests you have developed after the baby comes and as your family grows. You may not have as much time for them, but there is no reason for you to give them up completely.

NEWBORN INTENSIVE CARE UNIT

Most babies are born today healthy with almost certain chance for survival. However, about 10 percent of babies may have some risks to medical problems when they are born. There may be immaturity or some condition that requires special attention or very special care. Care of these higher risk babies requires doctors, nurses, and other trained personnel on a minute-to-minute basis. Therefore, in every part of the country, there are hospitals that have established intensive care nurseries, either called "newborn intensive care units" or "perinatal centers," to which babies who need this kind of care are sent as soon as the baby's doctor is aware of the need. Most hospitals have a staff able to care for most babies; however, babies requiring special care are brought either to the special unit or transferred to the center. Babies who have to be transferred are transported in specially equipped ambulance vehicles which contain all the necessary equipment to keep the baby's condition stable en route.

The most common cause for babies to go to this center is prematurity. Premature birth and the other illnesses and conditions that put babies at greater risk are quirks of nature and have many causes. Your doctor will talk with you about your baby's condition so that he can relieve any anxious feelings you may have. It is important for you to have all your questions answered.

In the center, your baby will be placed in a warmer bed or an incubator, providing an enclosed environment. In here, heat and moisture can be controlled and extra oxygen, if needed, can be supplied. An incubator also provides protection against infection. The entire nursery and the incubator is so designed that your baby can be easily observed for any signs of distress. Special wires are taped to your baby's skin to check the temperature constantly. Continuous monitoring of the heart and breathing rate is also done. Many of these small babies will require feeding, initially by intravenous techniques and then perhaps by a tube entering the stomach. But as the baby gains weight, he or she may nurse from a bottle or eventually breast-feeding. After a while, your baby will be well enough to move out of the intensive care nursery, and eventually, he will be ready to go home. Before your baby is discharged, you may want to spend several days in the nursery to make sure you know you can begin to provide for his or her care. It is important that you feel secure in starting to take care of your baby at home; therefore, don't hesitate to ask questions. You will then be ready to enjoy caring for your baby and watching the baby grow by giving him love and attention.

11
CONDITIONS ASSOCIATED
WITH PREGNANCY

The purpose of prenatal care is to watch for certain conditions of pregnancy which no one really likes to talk about, but which merit discussion. Knowing what they are and their danger signs will help you understand the nature of pregnancy and what can be done to ensure a successful outcome for mother and baby.

SPONTANEOUS ABORTION
OR MISCARRIAGE

Spontaneous abortion, more commonly known as "miscarriage," is the untimely termination of pregnancy usually before five months of pregnancy. The definition includes all fetuses weighing less than a pound at birth.

Miscarriage is always a traumatic event in any family and is often followed by depression in both parents. But it need not be. Spontaneous abortion is usually followed by another pregnancy which results in the birth of a healthy baby.

Causes of Abortion

A spontaneous abortion can result from one of three factors. There may be something wrong with the particular egg that was fertilized. Not all the seeds you plant in your garden grow. There may be something wrong with the sperm cell that fertilized a perfectly healthy egg. Or both cells may be perfectly all right, but something happens after they are joined that keeps the fertilized egg from growing properly. So, then, the cause of miscarriage could rest with any of the three parties involved—mother, father, or baby-to-be.

1. *Fetal cause*—Most miscarriages are caused by a failure of the fetus to develop well. One doctor proved this when he analyzed 1,000 pregnancies that ended in miscarriage. He found that 50 percent were caused by what is called the "blighted ovum." In these cases, the embryo starts to grow, then suddenly stops and dries up for no apparent reason, and the mother is left with an empty placenta. Another 10 percent of the cases studied were thought to be caused by a placenta that did not grow well and which would not, therefore, support pregnancy. While men often consider themselves the stronger sex, it is interesting to note that miscarriage of male fetuses is eight times more common than it is among females. Another fetal factor in miscarriage appears to be chromosomal abnormalities, which are 40 times more frequent in spontaneously aborted fetuses than they are in normal, full-term births.

2. *Maternal cause*—A small proportion of miscarriages are caused by a decrease in the production of the hormones that support pregnancy or by some abnormal condition in the uterus such as a small tumor. Thyroid conditions may also affect pregnancy outcome. Recently, some infections of the female reproductive tract have been implicated as the cause of repeated abortions. Surgical operation and mental or physical stress are not usually a cause for abortion. A rare cause is an abnormality of the reproductive tract, such as a double (bicornuate) uterus.

3. *Paternal cause*—Occasionally, the sperm which fertilized the egg is not strong enough to give the pregnancy a healthy start. This factor, however, is more difficult to pin down.

Diagnosis and Treatment

About 12 percent of all human pregnancies end in miscarriage, usually before the end of the first trimester. It happens in the best of families and has happened in mine twice. Yet, my wife is perfectly healthy, and we have four healthy daughters. Since the fetus is so vulnerable during the first few months, it seems likely that most miscarriages would occur then. And if it is going to happen, it is just as well to get it over with early to minimize the worry and anxiety of wondering whether or not everything will turn out well.

Once normal pregnancy has been diagnosed, any vaginal bleeding or pronounced pain in the lower abdomen are considered danger signs of possible miscarriage. This rule of thumb is a little exaggerated, however, since some 20 percent of all pregnant women who go to term experience some such bleeding. Though bleeding in itself does not necessarily mean impending abortion, it may be a warning signal. The association of lower abdominal cramps with continued vaginal bleeding may be a more definitive sign of impending miscarriage. Your doctor should be informed of any vaginal bleeding.

The treatment of a threatened miscarriage is very individual and depends on the woman and her physician. The classic treatment is restricted sexual activity and bed rest. Some doctors use vitamins, thyroid hormones and sedatives as well. The use of certain hormones is controversial at this time.

While bed rest and drugs are routinely used as treatment, they are the subject of controversy among many practicing obstetricians today. If we accept the figure that two-thirds of all abortions are inevitable because of the growth pattern of the fetus, then bed rest and other therapies can potentially help save only one-third of the group.

There is currently no way to accurately say when vaginal bleeding will result in miscarriage. If you experience such bleeding, your doctor may examine you weekly during the early phases of pregnancy to check the growth of the baby and placenta. He will also check to make certain the cervix is not dilating. If this happens, then the threat passes into an inevitable stage. Once the inevitable stage is reached, it is best to terminate the pregnancy by drugs or by a D & C, in which the doctor dilates the cervix and scrapes the uterine wall clean with an instrument. This is called "curettage."

The recent use of ultrasound in cases of threatened abortion has proven to be of great value. A reasonable estimate of fetal viability can be made and appropriate management can be carried out. Serial sonograms will also aid in following the development of the pregnancy. The serial use of quantitative blood pregnancy hormone measurements can also be of value in determining whether or not a pregnancy will end in miscarriage. A healthy viable pregnancy will have increasing levels of pregnancy hormones during the first 3 to 4 months of pregnancy. This test is called a quantitative beta-subunit HCG pregnancy test.

Sometimes after a spontaneous abortion, a piece of the placenta remains in the uterus, causing the signs of pregnancy to continue. This incomplete abortion is accompanied by continued vaginal bleeding and is best treated with dilatation and curettage.

Some miscarriages, usually of the later stages (14 to 20 weeks), occur because the mother's cervix will not stay closed to keep the baby in. This condition is called "cervical incompetency," and can be corrected by a very simple procedure. The doctor will sew a gathering stitch around the perimeter of the cervix, draw it tight and tie it. This "pursestring suture," as it is called, is left tied until the onset of labor, when it is removed to allow the birth of the baby.

Like all other facets of birth, miscarriage has many superstitions surrounding it. There is, for example, no proof of the popular adage that abortion or bleeding is more likely to occur during the time of the missed period each month. Similarly, it is also not true that some women are prone to miscarriage. A recurrent factor producing miscarriage is present only in four out of a thousand women. Not until a woman has had three successive miscarriages without a live birth is she a candidate for a medical workup to find out what the problem is. The rest of miscarriages can be attributed to random factors, which were discussed earlier.

An examination for habitual abortion (three or more) would consist of an x-ray of the whole reproductive system, called a "hysterogram," to make certain there is not a congenital abnormality or a growth in the uterus. Studies of the thyroid gland should also be performed to rule out the possibility of a basic hormonal problem.

Other possible causes of habitual abortion include genetic abnormalities in one parent, bacterial infections, and hormone deficiencies as well as the above.

A woman over 30 who has had two spontaneous abortions in a row should probably have the same medical evaluation as the so-called "habitual aborter."

Except for the few women who do have these problems, the overwhelming majority of women who have experienced spontaneous abortion can expect to be mothers of healthy babies in the future.

TOXEMIA OF PREGNANCY

Toxemia is probably the best-documented but least understood condition of pregnancy. It is seen only in pregnant human beings and is thought to be caused by a toxic agent that originates in the placenta, the kidneys, or both, though doctors are not certain of this. Since the last edition of this book, I am sorry to say we still do not know the cause of toxemia.

The condition is characterized by high blood pressure, fluid retention, and the presence of protein in the urine, usually during the third trimester. There are varying degrees of severity of this disease, though most cases are mild. General treatment requires early recognition for the potential for this disease. So doctors, during prenatal examinations, look for the predisposing factors of high blood pressure, kidney disease, multiple pregnancy, poor nutrition, and obesity. The incidence is higher among poor women.

Toxemia is a problem because it can cause a chemical environment in the mother's body which prevents the placenta from properly doing its job. Early detection and treatment of mild toxemia is the best way to keep severe problems from occurring. Precautions include a well-balanced diet to minimize weight gain. Early prenatal care is an important factor in its prevention. A good deal of rest is required for the toxemic mother, especially if she also has high blood pressure. If the latter condition persists, the doctor may prescribe some of the new pressure-reducing drugs that have been so successful lately. Many doctors like to admit toxemic women into the hospital before their due date to monitor them if toxemia becomes severe, and to prepare for early delivery so that the toxic agents in the mother's system do not interfere with the continued growth of the baby. Five decades ago, toxemia was a real problem. Today, however, with good prenatal care, the seriousness of toxemia has been reduced tremendously.

The use of nonstress test fetal monitoring, estriol tests, serial sonograms, and amniocentesis for fetal lung maturity have helped a great deal in our management of this complicated pregnancy.

DIABETES

Medical science has made it possible for a diabetic mother to go through pregnancy safely and have a healthy baby. Yet diabetes, a disorder in the body's use of sugars, should be closely monitored in pregnancy.

Babies of diabetic mothers tend to be larger than normal and tend to have a greater than normal incidence of hyaline membrane disease. The reason for the high birth weight of these babies is not understood, but one of the factors thought to be responsible is that the baby receives an excessive supply of sugar from the mother and produces excessive insulin.

Since very basic metabolic processes are involved in diabetes, pregnancy should be carefully monitored, if possible by a diabetic specialist or internist, and by a pediatrician in addition to an obstetrician. The dietary and insulin requirements of the pregnant diabetic should be carefully controlled to avoid insulin reactions and excessive weight gain. As a precaution, some diabetics are delivered before term to make certain serious complications do not develop. For those women who, through laboratory tests, show a potential for diabetes (so-called latent diabetes), a delivery of one or two weeks before term is sometimes recommended.

The use of fetal monitoring antepartum and amniocentesis are especially valuable in the care of these pregnancies.

Recent studies of diabetic pregnancies have shown that with very strict control of the maternal blood sugar level, a five-fold reduction in perinatal mortality could be attained.

RH DISEASE

Rh incompatibility occurs in 13 percent of all pregnancies. As explained in Chapter 6, Rh disease occurs in pregnancies in which the mother has Rh negative blood, and the father and the baby have Rh positive blood. The Rh factor is named for the rhesus monkey, a species of animal in whose blood it is always found. Humans who have the factor are Rh positive. Those who do not have it are Rh negative.

The problem can occur because, following the delivery of the placenta, a small amount of the baby's red blood cells spills into the mother's circulatory system. If the baby has the Rh factor and the mother does not, the mother will begin to build up permanent antibodies to the Rh factor, so that if a second baby is also Rh positive, the mother's antibodies will cross the placental barrier and systematically destroy the baby's blood. This may mean that the baby has to be given an exchange transfusion at birth to eliminate some of the toxic by-products of this blood destruction.

Rh disease, however, is on the way to eradication through the recent development of a vaccine called Rh immunoglobulin. Given within 72 hours of delivery, it prevents the mother from developing antibodies, so that a second Rh positive baby would not be growing in a hostile maternal environment. Rh immunoglobulin is almost 98 percent effective, but it must also be given after every spontaneous or elective abortion. It also should be given to Rh negative women who have amniocentesis, ectopic pregnancies, and possible bleeding in the third trimester. Your physician will advise you on this great advance in obstetrics. There are some centers that are also using Rh immunoglobin routinely at 28 weeks in unsensitized Rh negative women. This use is safe and does not hurt the fetus. This decreases the chances of sensitization from 2 percent to 0.2 percent. A second dose is also given after delivery.

The vaccine is not helpful to any mothers who became sensitized prior to the development of the vaccine. These women must still rely on developments such as amniocentesis and intrauterine transfusions. In intrauterine fetal transfusions, a needle is passed through the maternal abdomen into the uterus and into the baby's abdominal cavity, where blood is placed for transfusion. This was the first method for treating a sick fetus *in utero,* but its need has been diminished by the development of Rh immunoglobulin.

ECTOPIC PREGNANCY

An ectopic pregnancy is one in which the fertilized egg implants and grows outside the uterus, usually in the Fallopian tubes or ovaries. If passage of the egg is delayed in the tube by some blockage, which could have been caused by tubal infections, adhesions, or congenital blockage, the fertilized egg will implant there to develop. Since the uterus is the only human structure that can accommodate implantation and growth of a baby, the ectopic pregnancy is an ill-fated one which should be ended before the growing fetus causes the tube to rupture.

Ectopic pregnancy is characterized by a missed period followed by slight vaginal bleeding and pronounced pain on one side of the lower abdomen. If the doctor diagnoses ectopic pregnancy, he will probably remove the tube containing the misplaced fetus by abdominal surgery. Recently, some surgeons have been trying to save the affected tube by just removing the pregnancy. This is still somewhat controversial.

Chances for future pregnancies with just one tube after ectopic pregnancy are almost the same as they would be if it had never happened.

ABRUPTIO PLACENTAE

Abruptio placentae is the partial detachment of the placenta from the uterus before the baby is delivered. The condition is a problem because detachment interferes with the nutrition and respiration of the baby. If detachment is complete, the baby has no source of food and oxygen, and it dies.

Abruptio placentae usually makes itself known by bleeding, followed by sudden severe pain over the uterus.

A slight amount of premature separation is usually treated only by waiting. Often, a slight amount of separation is not diagnosed until after delivery, when a small blood clot is seen attached to the outer surface of the placenta.

Advanced separation is treated by early delivery, sometimes even by Cesarean section, if there is heavy bleeding.

PLACENTA PREVIA

Sometimes the fertilized egg implants itself too low in the uterus and partially blocks the cervical opening. This condition is known as "placenta previa." It becomes a problem late in pregnancy when the cervix begins to shorten, causing a partial separation of the placenta from the uterus, or abruptio placentae.

Coverage of the cervical opening may be partial or complete. It is characterized by painless vaginal bleeding in the last trimester, but can be positively diagnosed by vaginal examination in the operating room. At that point, Cesarean section may be required. In general, physicians try to delay treatment for this condition until after 37 weeks of gestation. Sonograms can be very helpful in the diagnosis and management of placenta previa.

Any significant vaginal bleeding in the third trimester of pregnancy should be immediately reported to your doctor.

PREMATURE RUPTURE OF MEMBRANES

Rupture of the membranes protecting the amniotic sac with leakage of amniotic fluid can occur at any time of pregnancy. If the baby is very premature, this results in potential problems. If the baby is close to term, problems are less important. Most often, rupture of the membranes occurs spontaneously and for unknown reasons.

The management of pregnancy once rupture of the membranes has occurred is still controversial. However, in the majority of cases, labor and delivery follows within a few days. If labor does not occur within 48 hours, the risk of infection then rises. Many obstetricians, for this reason, will induce labor if the pregnancy is close to term, and labor has not begun within 24 to 48 hours. However, if the infant is premature, induction of labor is not performed unless evidence of infection occurs.

If your water breaks and your physician decides to observe you, he will ask you to take your temperature frequently and report to him any temperatures over 100° F. He will ask you to refrain from sexual intercourse and tub baths and to keep in close touch with him. Many doctors will hospitalize their patients as well to observe the fetus and watch the mother more closely. With evidence of intrauterine infection, labor will be immediately induced or delivery will be accomplished by Cesarean section. In the absence of marked prematurity, most mothers and infants with this situation come out quite well.

HERPES INFECTIONS

Herpes simplex is a virus that causes infections in men and women. It is usually transmitted by sexual contact, especially the type II herpes virus which is almost exclusively in the genital tract. The virus causes lesions on the external genitalia which are painful and recurrent. The fetus and subsequently the infant can become infected with the virus if membranes are ruptured or as the fetus descends and is delivered through the vagina. Infection in the newborn can be very serious with some studies reporting a mortality rate of 60 percent. In view of the high degree of fetal and neonatal susceptibility, the following course of management has been suggested:

In the presence of active herpetic lesions on the maternal genitalia during labor, the infant should be delivered by Cesarean section. However, if the membranes have been ruptured for more than four hours, it is assumed that the virus has entered the amniotic cavity, and Cesarean section is no longer required. In the presence of a positive culture for herpes in the absence of lesions, the same course of treatment is still recommended. A woman who has had a history of these infections in the past should have cultures for herpes infections in the ninth month. Despite the fact that genital herpes has become more common in our society, the need for delivery by Cesarean is still quite rate. Herpes is not that common during pregnancy.

INTRAUTERINE GROWTH RETARDATION

Any infant that is born small for the gestational age, that is, the birth weight falls below the tenth percentile for his particular gestational age, is termed a growth retarded baby. The risk of fetal death and possible neurological and intellectual impairments goes up with growth retardation. The causes of fetal growth retardation are many: (1) poor maternal weight gain, (2) diseases of the blood vessels, such as pre-eclampsia and high blood pressure, (3) chronic kidney disease, (4) severe anemia, (5) smoking, (6) the use of hard drugs and alcohol during pregnancy, (7) multiple births, (8) fetal intrauterine infections, such as rubella, and (9) postmaturity. The diagnosis of intrauterine growth retardation depends on a careful history and a high suspicion if the presence of any of the above situations occur. Serial sonographic measurements of the fetus can aid in the diagnosis. Nonstress test antepartum fetal monitoring is also of value in determining when to deliver. With good obstetrical care, Intrauterine Growth Retardation can be prevented or appropriately managed.

PREMATURE LABOR

Most often, it is an advantage for a fetus to remain in the uterus until term. At times, however, he is better off being born even though early. An example of this would be a severely growth retarded fetus with a persistently hostile environment. An important problem is how we can best identify those fetuses which are better off being born even though they are preterm. Currently, there is great interest and conflicting opinions regarding the amount of interference the obstetrician should bring to the problem of preventing delivery before term.

Most often, the cause of labor before term is not known. A list of known causes of premature labor would include: (1) spontaneous rupture of membranes, (2) cervical incompetence, (3) uterine defects, (4) multiple births, (5) placenta previa and abruptio placentae, (6) serious maternal disease. However, most times, premature labor occurs spontaneously.

The diagnosis of premature labor can be definitely made if there is a change in dilatation of the cervix associated with uterine contractions. However, if uterine contractions are occurring at least once every ten minutes and last for 30 seconds for about an hour, this is usually diagnosed as premature labor.

We now have medications which quite effectively arrest premature labor. However, we must always ask "Is it beneficial or harmful to the fetus to remain in the uterus at this time?'' Your obstetrician must weigh many factors in the management of premature labor. The stage of pregnancy, the size of the fetus, certain adverse maternal conditions as causes for the premature labor are all important factors. If the decision to stop premature labor is made, currently the most effective drug is Ritodrine. This drug appears to be 60 to 70 percent effective in delaying the onset of labor for a significant portion of time.

POST-TERM PREGNANCIES

The post-term pregnancy is one that lasts for 42 weeks or more from the onset of the last menstrual period with a normal cycle of 28 days. The problem with making this diagnosis is that some of the actual post-term pregnancies are rather a result of an error in the estimation of the pregnancy stage. The value of precise knowledge of the stage of pregnancy is obvious. Early sonograms are a great help in accurately determining the stage of pregnancy. The majority of fetuses do well even though they stay in the uterus over 42 weeks. However, some fetuses run the risk of getting excessively large, making it harder to deliver, whereas other fetuses seem to outgrow their placentas and start to get thinner and not thrive. The use of estriol determinations, fetal nonstress testing and sonographic studies will aid in assuring a healthy outcome.

12
GENETIC FACTORS IN REPRODUCTION

The way your baby looks at birth and many of his physical and emotional characteristics in later life are determined by genetic factors in pregnancy. The goal of every pregnancy is the birth of a healthy child to a healthy mother. We have made great strides in achieving this goal. However, a small percentage of children are born with either major or minor birth defects, some of which are genetic or hereditary. The increased knowledge in the study of human genetics has changed the nature of modern obstetrical practice. Birth defects had always been a forbidden topic of discussion with expectant parents. However, the knowledge of human genetics coupled with such techniques as amniocentesis has made it possible to diagnose problems in pregnancy at a time to perform therapeutic abortion if the baby is found to have an incorrectible medical problem. These same methods, including ultrasound, are also used to confirm the nice aspects of pregnancy, such as the presence of twins.

Some genetic diseases can be treated or the health problems they cause can be lessened. Effective treatment for many genetic diseases, however, has not yet been found. However, advances have brought about the development of certain tests which may, for some genetic diseases, identify carriers of these diseases; persons who are not necessarily affected by the disease themselves but may be at risk of passing the disease to their children. There are also tests that can be performed during pregnancy to help determine the risk of genetic disease in the fetus.

Remember, the vast majority of babies are born healthy without any significant genetic disease. This chapter is not meant to frighten the reader about genetic disorders, but it is important for every expectant couple to be informed of genetic disease and aware of the availability of genetic counselling and testing if need be. The odds of having a genetic defect are small. Of course, the risk is different from couple to couple, but there are some groups of people who are considered at greater risk for genetic disorders. Every couple should review their families' past medical histories to see if they have any close relatives who had birth defects or mental retardation that could have been inherited. As previously discussed, older women are at a greater risk for certain types of chromosome abnormalities, and then there are the special genetic diseases that are more frequent in various ethnic or religious groups; for instance, sickle cell anemia, a genetic disorder of the red blood cell is found predominantly in blacks. Jewish persons from eastern European areas are more likely to have Tay-Sachs disease. Thalasemia, another blood disorder, is found most often in people of Greek and Italian heritage.

Actually, most people are believed to carry some defective genes. Normal genes are usually dominant over the defective ones, and these genes carrying the disorder can pass from generation to generation without ever producing a child with a defect. This so-called recessive gene may cause a defect only when both parents carry that same recessive gene. The parents themselves do not have to be afflicted with the disease to be carriers, but if both parents are carriers of the same recessive gene, the chances are 1 in 4 that a child will have a genetic disorder, and the odds are 1 in 2 that the child will be a carrier of the disease. Genetic diseases that are passed on by recessive genes include the diseases associated with ethnic or racial groups, such as sickle cell anemia and Tay-Sachs disease. Another example of recessive gene disease is cystic fibrosis.

A genetic disease may also be caused by a dominant gene, which means it takes only one parent to pass on the disease.

If a parent has a dominant gene for a disease, the chances are 50 percent that the baby will be born with that disease. An example of this type of disorder is Huntington's chorea, which affects its victims with muscle and speech disturbances.

The third group of genetic disorders are the so-called sex-linked or X-linked disorders. This abnormal gene is carried on the X chromosome. Remember, women have two X's; men, one X and one Y. Women can be carriers of these diseases, but only male children actually inherit and manifest the disease. If a woman is a carrier of one of the X-linked disorders, there is a 50 percent chance that any of her sons will have the disorder and a 50 percent chance that any of her daughters will be a carrier. The most well-known example of sex-linked disorders are hemophiliacs, who have abnormal bleeding tendencies, and certain types of muscular dystrophy.

Disorders may also be caused by a chromosome abnormality, some of which are inherited, but others which are caused by an isolated accident in the development of the fertilized egg. Each chromosome carries thousands of genes. The absence of a portion of chromosome material or the presence of an extra chromosome can cause serious consequences. Newborns with chromosome imbalances have mental retardation in addition to other defects. An example of this type of abnormality is Down's syndrome or mongolism, which will be discussed in detail below. The chances of conceiving a child with an extra chromosome, as in mongolism, increases with the age of the mother. For instance, only 1 in 1,600 children born to women in their twenties would have this problem, whereas in women over the age of 40, the risk is greater than 1 in 100. Some families carry a rearrangement of chromosome material called translocation which may cause a birth defect. The carrier of the translocation does not have the genetic disease itself, but the possibility of having a child with Down's syndrome may be as high as 5 to 10 percent. Remember, there are many birth defects which are not related to genes but are caused by health problems of the mother during pregnancy, such as virus infections, environmental factors, and poor nutrition.

GENETIC COUNSELLING

A couple going to genetic counselling after adequate workup will learn the mathematical chances of producing a child without genetic defects and whether there is a pattern of genetic disease. Genetic counselling may include tests and physical examination along with taking the family medical history. A thorough family medical history from both the male and female is very important. Examinations of each parent and their other children is also important since it may provide a clue to certain genetic abnormalities.

If a couple believes they are carriers of a genetic disorder, there are certain tests available to detect carriers of certain genetic disorders. Tests are available to detect carriers of diseases such as Tay-Sachs and sickle cell anemia, and communities may offer mass screening programs to peg persons in the high risk groups for these diseases. Another way carriers can be studied is through chromosome tests. Tests prepared from the patient's tissues are analyzed and a chart called a karyotype is worked out to demonstrate any chromosome abnormalities that may exist. Tests performed during pregnancy have already been discussed in the section on amniocentesis, which is the major test for genetic disorders in the unborn baby (see section on amniocentesis for further details).

If you are concerned about a genetic disorder, it is important to seek counselling so that correct information and risk factors can be evaluated prior to pregnancy. After determining risks, you can then decide whether or not to conceive a child. Amniocentesis can be performed during pregnancy in many instances so that the decision whether or not to continue a pregnancy can be determined. Amniocentesis may also pick up disorders that can be treated immediately after birth to avoid serious consequences. Even if a couple decides to continue an abnormal pregnancy, the knowledge of the risks in advance can be important, allowing them time to prepare themselves emotionally and medically.

Who should seek genetic counselling? (1) A woman over the age of 35 and pregnant, (2) a male over 55, (3) a couple who have already given birth to a child with genetic disease, (4) a couple with a family medical history of genetic disease, or (5) a couple from an ethnic or racial group in a high risk for genetic disorder.

Your physician can counsel you as to the best source for genetic counselling. There are many genetic centers now affiliated with major medical centers throughout the country. There are also a number of local and national organizations, such as the National Foundation of the March of Dimes, which can advise you as to the best source of counselling.

Some genetic effects and their risk factors in a subsequent pregnancy are listed in Table I.

TABLE I

Genetic Effects	Incidence in Population	Risk Figure in Subsequent Pregnancy
Twinning	1 in 89	1 in 89
Mongolism	1 in 600	1 in 20
Cleft palate	1 in 2,500	1 in 7
Harelip	1 in 1,000	1 in 7
Clubfoot	1 in 1,000	1 in 30
Congenital hip dislocation	1 in 1,500	1 in 20
Congenital heart disease	1 in 200	1 in 50
Pyloric stenosis	1 in 350	1 in 17
Cystic Fibrosis	Not known	1 in 4
Tay-Sachs disease	Rare	1 in 4
Sickle cell anemia	1 in 50 blacks	1 in 4

Multiple Pregnancy

Twins, triplets, quadruplets, etc., are always a source of interest to the parents, the physician, the community at large. Twins are born in 1 out of every 89 deliveries. Triplets occur in 1 in 16,666 births, quadruplets in 1 in 718,000 births.

About one-third of all twins are identical, which means they are formed from one fertilized egg which split and developed separately. The remainder of the twins are fraternal, which means they were formed by two separate eggs individually fertilized. Such twins would be as different as any two siblings.

There is evidence that both types of twinning are at least partially inherited. This tends to be supported by the way in which twinning is distributed in the population at large.

Twinning is more prevalent in the black population of America than it is in the white population, and triplets are twice as prevalent in blacks as in whites. The amount of twinning is different in different countries. It is most prevalent in Finland and least prevalent in Japan.

The genetic effect of multiple pregnancy is becoming blurred with the increased use of fertility drugs such as clomiphine and human menopausal gonadotropin in treating women who have been unable to conceive. These drugs increase the incidence of multiple pregnancy by stimulating multiple ovulation.

Marriage of Relatives

Since bad physical characteristics as well as good ones tend to run in families, marriage of relatives is generally discouraged. The incidence of congenital abnormality is twice as high when relatives marry as it is for the population at large, since it is more likely that the child will inherit two genes for a family disorder than if his parents did not come from the same family. For this reason, many states have laws prohibiting relatives closer than second cousins from marrying.

Down's Syndrome

In 1866, Dr. Langdon Down identified a small group of mentally defective children and called their condition "mongolism." It is only recently that the cause of Down's syndrome, as it is now called, has been discovered.

The disorder is caused by an extra chromosome in the baby which drastically alters the way the child develops. Diagnosis can be made by clinical examination and chromosomal analysis. This chromosomal error may arise by chance in normal parents, but its incidence rises with advancing maternal age. It is estimated that the risk of having a mongoloid child increases from 1 in 1,600 at puberty to 1 in 45 at menopause. The general frequency, regardless of age, is about 1 in 600 births.

Only about two percent of all Down's syndrome babies are inherited from the parents and are not influenced by maternal age. The theoretical risk of such a woman having a second mongoloid child in a subsequent pregnancy is one chance in three. Ninety-eight percent of all mongolism is of the spontaneous type (47 chromosomes instead of 46) and is directly age-related (see Table II).

TABLE II
INCIDENCE OF DOWN'S SYNDROME
WITH MATERNAL AGE

Age	Incidence
Under 25	1 in 1,600
25 to 35	1 in 600
35 to 40	1 in 150
40 to 45	1 in 100
Over 45	1 in 45
All mothers	1 in 600

The chapter on perinatology gives information pertinent to the antepartum diagnosis by amniocentesis of this disorder.

Ethnic Disorders

In addition to the genetic disorders which occur in the population at large, there are certain disorders specific to particular ethnic groups.

One of the most prevalent is sickle cell anemia, which affects American blacks predominantly, but not exclusively. Sickle cell anemia is an incurable disorder of the blood protein hemoglobin which causes normally round red blood cells to "sickle" when they are deprived of oxygen. Since this chain of events also inhibits the oxygen-carrying capacity of the red cells, the body cells and tissues can suffer oxygen deprivation and the hard sickle-shaped cells clog small capillaries, causing clots and severe pain.

About 1 in 50 black Americans has inherited two genes for this disorder and is said to have sickle cell anemia. One in ten black Americans has one gene for the disorder and is said to have the sickle cell trait. For the most part, those with the trait are symptom-free and lead absolutely normal lives. Premarital screening can pick up the carrier state.

People of Mediterranean ancestry suffer from Cooley's anemia, or thalasemia. There are two forms of this disorder—a major and a minor form—each of which also has a carrier or trait phase.

Cooley's anemia is also a disorder of hemoglobin and it requires periodic transfusions of whole blood for its victims. It, too, is incurable. Its incidence in closely knit Italian and Greek communities is about half that of sickle cell anemia in the black population.

People of Jewish ancestry are plagued by Tay-Sachs disease, which is caused by a deficiency of an enzyme on a genetic basis. This condition can be diagnosed while the fetus is *in utero* by amniocentesis when there is a previous family history. Pre-marital or pre-conceptual screening for the carrier state is indicated.

Cystic Fibrosis

This is a genetic disease causing alterations in digestion, respiratory function, and other systems of the children affected. Parents who have had one affected child have a 25 percent chance of each subsequent child being affected.

Pyloric Stenosis

This disorder is a digestive problem in which the newborn infant has a blockage in the digestive tract which causes him to vomit everything he eats. It is treated by surgical removal of the blockage. There is a possibility that subsequent babies in the same family will have the same problem. Male infants have one chance in ten to have it. Subsequent females have one chance in fifty.

13
ENVIRONMENTAL FACTORS IN PREGNANCY

There are certain exposures and experiences that the fetus can have *in utero* which can affect its future health and well-being. These external factors, some of which are quite hazardous, can be avoided by knowledge and proper care. Some of these factors actually are important prior to pregnancy; for instance, a woman should not become pregnant for three months following a rubella vaccination because of the possibility that live virus will be present following the vaccination which can affect a subsequent pregnancy. We also advise women not to become pregnant for three months following cessation of birth control pills. It appears that there is a slightly increased risk of abortion and miscarriage if conception occurs prior to three months. These are so-called preconceptional factors. A list of post-conception factors would include exposure to x-ray, exposure to drugs, exposure to viruses, exposure to chemical agents, and toxic effects from cigarette smoking.

RADIATION AND X-RAY

Almost weekly, our office receives a call from an expectant mother asking whether she can have dental x-rays. She has heard that radiation may cause damage to the fetus. In actuality, these types of x-rays can be performed if lead shielding is placed over the abdomen.

What are the actual facts about radiation? Exposure to radiation, such as x-rays, can have an effect prior to conception or following it. X-rays of the reproductive organs may cause chromosomal damage which may not be evident for several generations. In this case, an environmental condition can become inherited since the dose of radiation causing these gene mutations has not been determined. All x-ray to reproductive cells is considered dangerous and should not be performed unless necessary.

Radiation during pregnancy may be hazardous if a certain minimal dose is achieved. The hazards of dental and chest x-rays in relationship to the health benefits gained are minimal if properly performed. Excess radiation of the unborn fetus greater than 5 to 10 rads may cause malformations or eventual leukemia, especially when exposure occurs in the first trimester. In order to eliminate any risk caused by radiation, the following precautions are recommended:

1. The ovaries and testes should be protected from x-rays whenever possible.
2. Men should avoid conception for two months following x-rays of the testes.
3. Only essential x-rays should be taken after conception, and this should be done after shielding the uterus.
4. Married women of childbearing age should have elective x-rays only during the two weeks following the onset of the last menstrual period to avoid x-ray exposure of the fertilized egg before a diagnosis of pregnancy is possible.

Recent development of sonography has eliminated many of the indications for diagnostic x-rays during pregnancy. In addition, the use of x-ray pelvimetry, which is a measurement of the pelvic dimensions of the mother, has been decreased in the last five years as well. There are not many indications for x-rays during pregnancy, and obstetricians are well aware of radiation's two-edged sword during pregnancy and use it with caution.

INFECTIONS

The possible hazardous effect of maternal German measles (rubella) on the fetus has been well documented. Exposure to the virus in the first half of pregnancy is most dangerous and can result in heart disease, deafness, or central-nervous-system damage in the newborn. The chance of such damage is at least 30 percent if a mother contracts the infection during the first or second trimester.

A good vaccine for rubella has been developed, and all children should be vaccinated. So should women of childbearing age if there is no possibility of pregnancy existing at the time the injection is given and no expectation of pregnancy for at least three months after the vaccine is administered.

Another infection of late pregnancy has been shown to cause birth defects. This infection, called "toxoplasmosis," is an organism found in raw meat and in the feces of animals that eat raw meat.

To avoid the hazard, a pregnant woman, especially in her last trimester, should refrain from eating such delicacies as steak tartare, and should let another family member clean the kitty-litter pan for the period of gestation. A blood test for toxoplasmosis is available during pregnancy.

CHEMICAL AGENTS

The possible risk of drugs in pregnancy was painfully dramatized in 1962 when the excellent tranquilizer, Thalidomide—popular in Europe—was shown to cause about 5,000 cases of phocomelia, or immature limb development in newborn babies.

The greatest lesson of that tragedy was that all drugs must be tested on pregnant animals of different species at different periods of gestation before they can be approved for use among pregnant women. And since the results of animal studies are not directly applicable to humans, any use of drugs, especially early in pregnancy, is taking a chance.

A woman must learn this, since much fetal growth occurs before she would be aware of pregnancy and elect to stop taking it.

A recent study showed that an average woman takes four

different kinds of medication during pregnancy. Aspirin, antihistamines, tranquilizers, laxatives, nasal decongestants, and antivomiting agents led the list.

In each case, a woman and her doctor must balance the need for the drug against its possible effect on the baby. Of course, that effect will depend upon dosage, the woman's sensitivity to that particular chemical agent, and the point in gestation at which it is administered.

Table III shows a list of some commonly used drugs and their known effect on developing babies. It is meant to be a general guide rather than a list of what you should or should not take during pregnancy. This must be determined by your doctor.

There is currently much discussion about the effects of certain illegal drugs on pregnancy. LSD is said to cause chromosomal damage. Heroin use during pregnancy causes addicted babies. Marijuana is not recommended during pregnancy as well.

Other environmental factors would include smoking and alcohol which have been discussed previously in another chapter.

TABLE III
EFFECTS OF SOME DRUGS ON THE FETUS

Drug	Effect
Thalidomide	Phocomelia
Smoking	Prematurity and small infants
Quinine	Abortion or bleeding problem
Tetracycline	Decrease in bone growth and discoloration of teeth
Sulfonamides (sulfa) late in pregnancy	Newborn jaundice
Vitamin K in excess	Neonatal hemorrhage
Aspirin in excess	Neonatal hemorrhage
Chloromycetin	Fetal death
Vaccination	Fetal vaccination
Dicoumerol	Fetal death
Diuretics in excess	Fetal chemical imbalance, placental insufficiency
Testosterone	Virilization
Stilbestrol	Vaginal cancer in female offspring
Streptomycin	Nerve damage
Librium	Defects
Dilantin	Defects

14
PREVENTING PREGNANCY (CONTRACEPTION, ABORTION, AND STERILIZATION)

CONTRACEPTION

It is not until the baby is born and settled in the household that an old problem pops up—contraception. There are several effective contraceptive methods to choose from, until you decide to have another baby. These should be discussed with your physician as to the best method for you as an individual.

Oral Contraceptives

The development of the oral contraceptive, or "the pill," as it is commonly known, is one of the great scientific achievements of the past two decades. The pill is the closest thing available to an ideal contraceptive. It is 100 percent effective when taken as instructed. It is easily reversible when children are desired, and it is inexpensive.

In 1960, the United States Food and Drug Administration authorized the marketing of the birth-control pill called Enovid. A whole generation of women have used it and its successors effectively. It has produced quite an impact on our society.

There are certain difficulties, however, associated with

"the pill," the greatest of which is remembering to take it every day. Other drawbacks include side effects, especially in the early months of usage, but these usually go away as the body adapts to the hormonal changes. These hormonal changes in rare cases are known to cause problems such as blood clotting and even death.

Nevertheless, on the basis of current available knowledge, the benefits of oral contraceptives far outweight their potential dangers. The dangers of pregnancy and childbirth may outweigh the dangers of taking the pill, and there are many other drugs commonly used, such as penicillin, which can be more dangerous than "the pill."

Oral contraceptives contain synthetic hormones which are taken in various combinations for 21 days of the menstrual cycle. Basically, all pills contain a combination of both estrogen and progesterone type hormones. The quantities of estrogen and progesterone have been altered during the past ten years so that currently there are available pills which contain minute amounts of these agents. The hormones in the pill, when taken for 21 days, produce an inhibition of ovulation. Without ovulation, pregnancy cannot occur. In addition, the hormones in the pill cause other changes which make pregnancy unlikely. Progesterone causes the cervical mucus to become thick and impenetrable to the sperm, thereby preventing them from entering the uterus. In addition, the lining of the uterus is altered hormonally, making it unreceptive to a possible fertilized egg.

Despite its relative safety, no woman should take the birth-control pill without a gynecologic checkup, a breast examination, and a Pap smear. A complete history must also be taken before the pill is prescribed. Women with a history of blood clots or embolism, strokes, heart disease, serious liver disease, or unexplained bleeding from the vagina should not take the pill. Also, if there is a history of high blood pressure, diabetes, epilepsy, migraine headaches, serious mental disturbances, visual problems, or kidney disease, the pill should not be taken. Your doctor is the best one to advise you about the safety of the pill in your individual case. You and he can arrive at the decision balancing the risk against the benefits.

When pregnancy is desired, the oral-contraceptive effect is

easily reversible once the pill is stopped. The woman finishes her pill series and does not start another series. The pregnancy rate after the cessation of oral contraceptives is the same as the rate in women who have never taken the birth-control pill. That is, 90 percent of women will become pregnant within one year of trying to do so. Babies born to women who have used oral contraceptives show no after-effects from the medication. After stopping the pill, it is best to avoid pregnancy for three normal cycles because of a slightly high spontaneous abortion rate if conception occurs during this period. There is a small group of women who, having stopped taking the pill, experience a delay in ovulation and menstruation for a number of months. In rare cases, this has been for as long as a year. This condition is called "post-pill amenorrhea" or lack of menstruation and occurs usually in women who had irregular menstrual cycles before taking the pill. It can be treated, however, by the use of other medications which can bring on ovulation, menstruation, and pregnancy.

There are side effects which are common in women taking the pill. The majority of women, however, taking the low-dose contraceptives do not experience any side effects or are bothered by only mild, transient effects. Psychological factors seem to play some part in the incidence of these effects. Nausea is common during the first couple of cycles and usually can be avoided by changing the time of day that the pill is taken, from morning to midday. Fluid retention may be a problem, as may bloating, swelling of the legs, and weight gain. This can be treated by a low-salt diet or by diuretics, if necessary. Other occasional, minor changes are an increase in vaginal discharge and increase in facial pigmentation, especially when exposed to strong sunlight. This pigmentation change is reversible on stopping the pill. Other women experience some mild mood changes including depression, as well as changing appetite and weight gain. Breast enlargement is also common during the early cycles of taking the pill. Breakthrough bleeding or spotting between menstrual periods is another common side effect, which usually disappears after the third cycle. If this is persistent, a higher dose of medication can be prescribed. Recurring vaginitis, or vaginal infection, is common among women on the pill, especially infections caused by an organism called "yeast fungus." This condition should be treated by your doctor.

There are occasionally serious complications associated with pill usage, such as blood clots in veins and possibly an embolus or traveling blood clot in the lungs. Even though there is a greater risk of blood clot in women taking the pill, the death rate from clots caused by the pill is only 4 percent per 100,000 users among all ages. There is no evidence of cancer resulting from the use of the birth-control pill. Some recent studies have suggested that there is a lower risk of ovarian cancer occurring in women who have been on the birth-control pill in past years.

Intrauterine Devices

The effectiveness of the intrauterine device to prevent conception has been known for over 2,000 years. Turkish camel drivers inserted small round pebbles into the uteri of their camels centuries ago before going into the desert to prevent the camels from becoming pregnant during the long journey. Hippocrates, the ancient Greek doctor, even placed an intrauterine device into the womb of a woman to prevent pregnancy.

During the past 25 years, doctors have devoted serious attention to perfecting intrauterine devices which are placed inside the uterus and left there.

There are many conflicting theories as to how the IUD works. Its exact mode of action is still not understood. The three main theories are that (a) it changes the muscle balance of the uterus and Fallopian tubes; (b) it changes the lining of the uterus, called the "endometrium," which prevents the implantation of the fertilized egg into the lining; and (c) it alters the chemical environment of the uterus, preventing fertilization and implantation.

The new synthetic plastics which are flexible and moldable are being used for intrauterine devices. These plastic devices do not react with body chemicals. They are malleable and therefore easy to insert.

Recently small amounts of pure copper have been added to the plastic devices to improve the effectiveness of the device.

In order to evaluate an IUD, its expulsion rate, failure rate, and side effects must be considered. Most of the IUDs have a 1 to 2 percent pregnancy rate over a year's use. Another 10 percent of women spontaneously expel the IUD, and another 10 percent of women have the device removed because of troublesome side effects. Therefore, it appears that the IUD will be successful or tolerated by only about 80 percent of women.

Insertion of an IUD is usually a simple, rapid, and more or less painless procedure. It is inserted following a complete examination, usually during or immediately following a menstrual period. It is introduced into the uterus, leaving some nylon threads protruding into the upper vagina. These strings are left so the woman may check to make certain it has not been expelled and to allow for removal without difficulty. The IUD is effective immediately following insertion, and neither the male nor the female should be aware of its presence after insertion. Women who have never been pregnant tolerate the IUD less well than do women who have had children. They tend to experience a greater degree of pain on insertion and immediately after insertion of the IUD. Women who have had children have a greater expulsion rate and a higher incidence of cramps during the first couple of menstrual cycles after insertion. Minor side effects of the IUD are also common but not serious. These side effects will often disappear after a few months' use. They include increased menstrual cramps, severe irregular bleeding during the month— that is, spotting—and occasionally very heavy menstrual flow.

The intrauterine device should be checked periodically by your physician, probably every six months. Serious complications are possible with the IUD; they include pelvic infection and possible uterine perforation. The risk of serious pelvic infection is 1 to 2 percent in some series. These infections can lead to sterility. This factor should be considered in your choice of IUD. I believe that uterine perforation most often occurs upon insertion; and once the IUD is properly inserted, its passage into the abdominal cavity would be quite unusual.

The IUD is less efficient than the pill, since the pregnancy rate is 1 to 2 percent during a full year's use. For unknown reasons, the IUD appears to be most effective in women who have had several children and are over 30 years of age.

The IUD is still one of the best contraceptive methods available. It is safe, easy to use and inexpensive, requires only an initial insertion, and is therefore indefinitely effective, and does not interfere with the enjoyment of sexual intercourse. Its contraceptive effect is completely reversible when it is removed, and pregnancy may be undertaken again. It is probably best for women who have completed childbearing.

The Condom

The condom is a sheath worn on the penis during sexual intercourse. It is a widely used, effective mechanical contraceptive. The condom is made of strong latex rubber. It is readily available and reliable. Its disadvantage is that it is used by the man alone, making the woman completely dependent upon her male partner for contraception. Another drawback is that it interferes with the spontaneity of sex. On the plus side, the condom is completely harmless and simple to use. It is a good birth-control method for occasional or unexpected sexual intercourse. In addition, it provides some protection against venereal diseases such as syphilis and gonorrhea.

The condom is the most commonly used mechanical contraceptive, and one report suggests that over 750 million condoms are sold every year on this continent. No prescription is required to purchase a condom.

The Diaphragm-Jelly Method

A popular and effective mechanical form of birth control is the diaphragm, used with a spermicidal jelly. The diaphragm is a round disk made of soft rubber, stretched around a circular spring. It is inserted into the vagina prior to sexual relations and maintains a physical barrier between the sperm and the cervix. The spermicidal preparation that is smeared on the diaphragm prior to insertion kills sperm which might pass around the edge of the diaphragm or remain in the vagina.

The diaphragm must be individually fitted by a doctor, who will write a prescription for its purchase. Any woman can be fitted for a diaphragm; however, certain women have to be very careful with its use and insertion. Childbirth may change the size and shape of the vagina, requiring a new fitting. Upon fitting of the diaphragm, the doctor will teach you how to use it. The diaphragm can be inserted up to two hours before sexual intercourse and should remain in place at least six hours following intercourse. A woman can walk around, bathe or urinate with the diaphragm in place. After an act of sexual intercourse, an additional application of spermicidal cream or jelly must be inserted before each additional coitus. Douching is unnecessary following removal of the diaphragm. The diaphragm can also be used during menstruation; however, conception is highly unlikely at that time anyway. If positioned correctly, the diaphragm cannot be felt by either the male or the female during sexual relations. The diaphragm is approximately 95 percent effective when used. Human frailty is the main reason for its potential failure.

Vaginal Spermicides

The use of a sperm-killing agent placed inside the vagina prior to sexual intercourse is an old method of birth control. Over the ages, different preparations have been used as vaginal contraceptives. Today, many chemical agents are available. They consist of foams, creams, jellies, and tablets. The most effective appears to be the foam, since once inserted into the vagina, it spreads quickly and evenly over the cervix and forms a chemical barrier to penetration of the sperm through the cervix. The creams, jellies, and tablets are less likely to spread properly over the cervix. In addition, the foam is less messy with leakage from the vagina. The foams are bought without prescription. The failure rate of foams may be as high as 10 percent, so for a mechanical form of birth control, they are not as effective as the diaphragm and condom.

The Rhythm Method

The rhythm method of birth control is the abstinence from sexual intercourse on those days of the menstrual cycle when the woman is most likely to become pregnant. This is not an effective birth control method, but may be the only method available to some women because of religious beliefs. Women who must not become pregnant should not rely on this method. It cannot be used by any woman who has irregular cycles.

The method depends on the fact that conception occurs near the time of ovulation, and ovulation usually occurs 14 days before the onset of the next menstrual flow. Therefore, conception is least likely at the beginning and end of the menstrual cycle and most likely in midcycle. In order to use the rhythm method, a woman should keep a record of her menstrual cycles for eight months. When a pattern is clear, the first day of menstrual flow is designated day 1. To calculate the unsafe period, she subtracts 18 from the length of the shortest cycle to find the first unsafe day, and then subtracts 11 from the longest menstrual cycle for the last unsafe day. A woman must not have intercourse from the first unsafe day through the last unsafe day. The woman must also continue to record the length of each cycle and base her calculations on the last eight cycles.

Another rhythm method of birth control that does not rely upon calendar alone includes temperature taking. A woman's body temperature is higher during the second part of her menstrual cycle. This increase in temperature is caused by the release of the hormone progesterone following ovulation. To use this method, a woman takes her temperature before getting out of bed each morning. This temperature is known as the "basal body temperature," BBT. Special thermometers with fine gradations are available to determine basal body temperature accurately. By recording basal body temperature daily, it can be assumed that three days after the rise in basal body temperature, ovulation is completed, and the safe period has begun. The unsafe period cannot be determined except by the calendar method. The combination of the temperature and calendar methods can shorten the unsafe period. The first unsafe day is calculated from the shortest cycle as outlined above. The last unsafe day is the third day after the rise in basal body temperature.

Coitus Interruptus or Withdrawal

Withdrawal is one of the oldest methods of birth control known, but it is difficult to use properly and has a very high failure rate. When this method is used, sexual intercourse continues until just before male orgasm. When the male feels ejaculation coming, he withdraws his penis from the vagina, preventing the emission of the sperm into the vagina.

As a technique, it has several problems. It relies upon the male partner and his will power. It may not work because some sperm may be ejaculated in small amounts prior to orgasm. Coitus interruptus is a physically harmless method, but it can cause psychological problems. With the existence of cheap, easily available mechanical and hormonal contra-

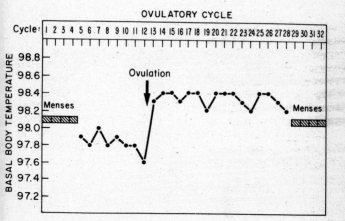

Figure shows the basal body temperature during a normal ovulation menstrual cycle. Note that ovulation occurs before the rise in temperature. The BBT can be used for both fertility and contraceptive purposes.

ceptives, this method should not be considered a valuable birth-control technique.

There are other methods suggested for birth control that do not work. Douching is absolutely worthless, whether with water, Coca-Cola, or 7-Up. Saran Wrap is not a substitute for a condom. In addition, breast-feeding is not an absolute contraceptive method.

Morning-After Pill

Scientists are currently working to develop a pill to prevent the implantation of a fertilized egg following contraceptive failure. The pill is commonly called the "morning-after pill."

Various types of medications have been tested; one type of morning-after pill consists of a large dose of the hormone estrogen administered within three days after unprotected intercourse. It results in a shedding of the uterine lining, so that the egg cannot implant. Its side effects limits its general use. Other safer types are being studied.

ELECTIVE ABORTION

Elective abortion is becoming an increasingly available alternative to contraceptive failure. In January 1973, the Supreme Court legalized abortion in the United States. In states where laws had been changed, the maternal death rate had dropped, as had the illegitimacy rate and the infant mortality rate. The decision to have an abortion is between a woman and her doctor.

There are several kinds of abortion techniques, the use of which is usually determined by the stage of pregnancy.

D & C (Dilation and Curettage)

The D & C is probably the oldest of the abortion techniques used today. It consists of dilating the cervix and scraping the uterus clean. It is performed under local or general anesthesia up to the twelfth week of pregnancy. The D & C is also used to "clean out" the uterus following a spontaneous abortion or miscarriage.

Vacuum Aspiration

The more common technique used today is the vacuum suction technique. It too requires a slight dilation of the cervix, after which an instrument called a "suction cannula" is held in the uterus. The cannula is attached to a pump which suctions out the contents of the uterus like a vacuum cleaner. This method is also confined to the first 12 weeks of pregnancy. It is widely used because it results in only a small loss of blood and it is less likely to damage the uterus. It is the quickest and simplest of the abortion techniques. It can be performed using local anesthetics in an office or out-patient operating room.

Late Abortion Techniques (After 14 Weeks)

After 14 weeks, abortion techniques change. Generally, two methods are available. One is called a D & E (dilatation and evacuation). It involves the dilatation of the cervix large enough to allow special instruments to be inserted to evacuate the uterine contents manually. Suction is also used in this method.

The other technique involves the injection of certain substances into the uterine cavity to produce labor. Amniotic fluid is usually removed and substances, such as salt solutions, urea, or a chemical called prostaglandin is instilled. Labor usually occurs within 8 to 12 hours, and the fetus and placenta are passed spontaneously. Some states allow this type of abortion up to 24 weeks of gestation.

Hysterotomy

This method is the least commonly used of all. It requires surgical incision into the uterus, the same approach used for Cesarean section. This method is usually reserved for second-trimester abortion in which the other methods have failed, or for an abortion accompanied by sterilization procedure, such as a severing of the Fallopian tubes.

Factors in Abortion

While moral and theological considerations may delay a decision to seek an abortion, abortions are safer from a medical standpoint when performed between the sixth and tenth week of pregnancy.

For the woman seeking an abortion, there is certain basic information she should have. It is important that the patient seeking an abortion be certain she is pregnant. One abortionist who recently summarized his experience of a 25-year period said that 10 percent of the women who came to him were not pregnant. Many calls have been received from women seeking abortion who are only two days late with their menstrual flow. Many factors other than pregnancy can delay the onset of the period, such as weight change, anxiety, illness, travel, and normal variation in the cycle, and nothing really can be gained by rushing into an abortion as soon as a period is slightly delayed. Therefore, diagnosis is very important prior to seeking an abortion. The new blood pregnancy tests are very accurate early in pregnancy.

The patient's physician is the best one to determine the diagnosis of pregnancy and recommend the best type of procedure. In addition, an examination by a competent physician may reveal that there are other problems in need of treatment in addition to or prior to an abortion. Occasionally, pregnancy may be in the Fallopian tube or there may be ovarian cysts or vaginal infections present.

Then, too, women who are aborted feel that there is no reason to see a doctor again. Occasionally, some problems, such as excessive bleeding and infection, force a woman to seek medical care; but under normal or common conditions, a woman might not see a doctor again. Occasionally, we see a woman who may still be pregnant despite an attempted abortion. Therefore, it is important that a postoperative examination be performed approximately 1 to 2 weeks following the operation. At the initial visit, after a medical checkup is performed, contraception can also be planned for. Following an abortion, a woman should think about developing a contraceptive plan.

Sterilization procedure, if desired, can also be combined with the abortion and should be planned for in advance.

The emotional after-effects of an abortion should not be forgotten. Some women will have an immediate response of relief; however, others suffer periods of depression with crying, fatigue, and insomnia. However, these are usually short-lived and not serious, and they pass. They are not very different from the postpartum or "baby blues" that many women experience after regular delivery.

Remember to get Rh immunoglobulin if you are Rh negative and have either a spontaneous or induced abortion.

STERILIZATION

Sterilization is a permanent surgical means of preventing pregnancy. It is often advised when another pregnancy would endanger the life of the mother or for parents who have children with genetic birth defects which have a strong possibility of showing up again.

Increasingly, however, couples are turning to sterilization once their family has reached optimal size. Female sterilization leaves the major organs of reproduction untouched. The most common method, tubal ligation, consists of cutting the Fallopian tubes and sewing them shut so that the egg never reaches the uterus to meet with sperm. The unfertilized egg disintegrates. The woman continues her normal menstrual cycle.

The operation is fairly simple and can be performed vaginally or through a small incision in the abdomen. If performed immediately following delivery, tubal ligation requires only an inch-and-a-half-length incision and a few days' stay in the hospital. In fact the operation can be performed immediately following delivery under the same anesthesia used for delivery. Performed at other times, the procedure is a little more of an operation.

Laparoscopy

More recently, other techniques using a procedure called laparoscopy have been developed for sterilization purposes. A laparoscope is a long tubelike instrument fitted with lights and mirrors that is inserted through a small incision, usually in the navel area of the abdomen. Through this instrument, the pelvic organs can be seen, including the tubes. The tubes are then either cauterized—that is, burned—or closed with a plastic band. Usually, general anesthesia is required for this procedure. However, some clinics are performing this on an out-patient basis under local anesthetics. The risks of the procedure are minimal. The main risks seem to be those related to the general anesthetic plus the rare complication of injury to the bowel or tissues by the cauterization. Current experience with laparoscopic tubal ligation has proven to be a safe and successful option. Laparoscopic technique requires a shorter hospital stay than the abdominal operation, sometimes only one day, and is usually less expensive.

Sterilization by tubal ligation does not affect the woman's menstrual or hormonal cycle. Ovulation will occur in the usual fashion, and the uterus will react normally to the cyclic ovarian hormones. Menstruation will take place, but the pathway for the egg and sperm combination has been interrupted and therefore pregnancy does not occur. Sexual responsiveness and orgasm are not affected by these techniques. Research is currently being carried out in many institutions on an even more simple out-patient sterilization procedure. One procedure includes an instrument called the hysteroscope which is another way of looking inside the endometrial cavity of the uterus. Techniques are being evaluated that close the entrance to the Fallopian tubes from the endometrial cavity, either permanently or temporarily. However, at this time, these procedures are still experimental.

Male Sterilization

Some men equate male sterilization with castration. This is not the case at all. The most common form of male sterilization used today is called "vasectomy."

Vasectomy involves cutting the sperm ducts in the testicle, preventing the passage of sperm to the penis. Sexual desire and activity should remain the same. The only observable difference will be a 10 percent decrease in the volume of ejaculate.

Vasectomy is easy to perform and can be done as an out-patient procedure under local anesthesia. A small incision is made in the scrotum over the sperm duct (the vas deferens), which is cut. It will then take about three weeks for all the sperm to leave the tract, completing the procedure. A semen sample should be examined under a microscope for sperm before the operation can be called completely successful.

Vasectomy carries with it a 1 percent failure rate, since

every once in a while, the two ends of the sperm duct rejoin and allow the flow of sperm through the penis. Attempts to restore fertility, however, are less than 50 percent successful.

15
INFERTILITY

Any book on pregnancy and childbirth should include a chapter on infertility. Reproduction is an essential aspect of most marriages, so that inability to conceive ranks high among the causes of marital unhappiness. Whether true or not, many people believe that a child is necessary for a strong family relationship.

The exact incidence of infertility is difficult to compute. We may define sterility or infertility as the inability to conceive after a year of trying. The primary form of sterility is that in which conception has never occurred. The secondary variety is one where previous conception has taken place, but a repeat attempt at conception has been unsuccessful. We may say a couple is absolutely sterile when it is clear that conception is impossible. This would be true if a woman has had a hysterectomy or if the man has no sperm in his semen. Many couples experience a relative sterility where factors are present which make conception difficult, though not impossible. It is estimated that 10 to 15 percent of marriages will have problems with conception.

The one-year definition outlined above is not an arbitrary one. Many analyses have shown that two-thirds of pregnancies occur within three months of initiation of unprotected intercourse. Within six months of trying to conceive, 75 to 80 percent of couples are successful, and by the end of one year, 80 to 90 percent have conceived. At the end of one year of fruitless attempts to have a baby, a couple should be regarded as candidates for a full-scale investigation to determine the cause of their trouble. At least 5 percent of normal women will conceive during the second year of trial. But a couple who have been unsuccessful after trying one year should seek medical help. Couples in their thirties or forties should wait somewhat less than one year before seeking medical advice.

ESSENTIAL FACTORS IN INFERTILITY

Before discussing the causes of infertility, it is necessary to review the mechanisms involved in normal reproduction. In every case of sterility, one or more of these mechanisms is altered:

1. The testicles must produce healthy sperm that are able to propel themselves to meet the female egg.
2. The ovaries must produce healthy eggs that must be discharged at ovulation at regular intervals.
3. The semen must be deposited at or near the cervix so the sperm can make their way toward the ovum, and, of course, this occurs by the male's satisfactory completion of sexual intercourse.
4. The ovum, after ovulation, must meet with no obstruction as it passes through the tube toward the sperm.
5. The sperm, likewise, must meet no physical or chemical obstruction as it passes through the cervix, into the uterus, and into the tube toward its meeting with the egg.
6. The fertilized egg must arrive in the uterus at the time when there is a ready site of implantation in the uterine wall.

Therefore, it is obvious that the causes of sterility can be either male or female in origin, so that a couple with a problem should seek medical advice and treatment together.

The doctor you choose will organize a diagnostic search and survey. This investigation begins with the first office visit, when a thorough family history is taken. Information concerning previous marriages, previous pregnancies, menstrual cycle, and sexual habits will be explored, and general physical examination and some laboratory studies will be performed.

There are probably five major factors the doctor will investigate:

1. Pelvic conditions such as tumors, infections, and anatomical variations should be ruled out. However, these abnormalities are uncovered in fewer than 5 percent of women.
2. The whole process of insemination will be explored, including impotence problems, how close to the cervix the semen is deposited, and failure of sperm to pass through the cervix because of a hostile chemical makeup of cervical mucus. This reaction can be detected by performing a Heuhner test on cervical secretion after intercourse. Surprisingly, this condition may be remedied by the use of condoms for a short period of time to remove the allergic reaction.
3. A tubal factor may be present. Partial or complete closure of the Fallopian tubes is determined by an x-ray examination of the uterus and tubes, called "hysterosalpingography." Laparoscopy has become a very useful tool in the evaluation of tubal and pelvic factors. Direct visualization of the pelvis can document such problems as chronic infection, adhesions, endometriosis, and ovarian disease.
4. The endocrine factor in the female may be a problem, causing alterations in menstruation and ovulation, or inadequate preparation of the endometrium (the uterine wall) for implantation of the fertilized egg. This factor is evaluated by performing endometrial biopsies, by taking the basal body temperature, and by hormonal studies of various types.
5. A problem with the male reproductive tract accounts for infertility among 40 percent of couples studied. This factor is investigated by examination of the semen, usually performed by a urologist.

If a combination of two or more of these five factors exists, the probability of successful conception is reduced. Multiple faults are found in more than 60 percent of couples with primary and secondary sterility. The investigation and treatment of these five major factors are the mainstay of the management of this problem.

Another aim of the sterility investigation, besides enabling a couple to bear children, is to determine the chances of eventual pregnancy. This permits the couple to have an intelligent outlook on the problem and to adjust and make plans concerning the possibility of adoption or artificial donor insemination.

The chance of successful pregnancy following infertility evaluations and therapy is estimated to be between 20 and 50 percent. In general, one out of every three couples who seek medical help following one year of inability to conceive will be successful in having a baby. This can be compared to the one out of 20 couples who will conceive during the second year of trying without seeking medical help. Therefore, it should be obvious that medical evaluation and therapy for the infertile couple can be a great help.

TREATMENT OF INFERTILITY

Treatment of the female factors in infertility depends on the cause. Abnormalities of the cervical factors can sometimes be treated with special douches, small doses of hormones, or treatment of any infection that might be present. Treatment of the uterine factors may depend on surgery or antibiotics. Treatment of tubal factors and pelvic factors may also depend on surgery. However, recently endometriosis has been successfully treated with a drug called "danocrine." This drug used for 6 to 8 months will cause endometriosis to dry up with subsequent pregnancy rates as high as 50 percent. Certain surgical procedures have been devised to re-establish the openness of the Fallopian tubes. Success in these techniques is as high as 50 percent in achieving pregnancy. The Fallopian tubes are extremely delicate structures, and the aim of the surgery is to produce a functionally open tube. This can sometimes be achieved by meticulous microscopic surgical techniques with very fine instruments and materials.

However, before undergoing tubal surgery, a woman must understand what the procedure is and what the likelihood of success will be. Success is eventually determined by subsequent pregnancy, not just by re-establishing an opening in the tube. The risk of ectopic pregnancy will also increase following this type of surgery.

Treatment of the hormonal factors usually centers around treatment of anovulation. Occasionally, an underactive thyroid gland can also be responsible for infertility. Failure to ovulate is a very complex problem and a frequent cause of infertility. Ovulation is a complex event requiring the functioning of the pituitary gland, the hypothalamus of the brain, the ovary and the uterus in synchrony. In the past ten years, the development of certain drugs to induce ovulation has proven to be a great boon to treating infertility. The prime reason for attempting to restore ovulation is usually to produce conception. Anovulation, actually, is a normal characteristic of the early years and the later years of menstruation. In and of itself, anovulation is no problem, except if you are trying to conceive. There are basically two types of drugs now available and commonly used to produce ovulation. One is a chemical called clomiphene and the other involves the use of uterine hormones, namely pituitary gonadotropins.

Clomiphene, the "Fertility Pill"

Clomiphene is used in pill form and works by way of the brain and the pituitary to produce the release of gonadotropic hormones from the pituitary gland. In order for clomiphene to be effective, it is essential that estrogen secretion associated with the first half of the menstrual cycle be adequate and that a woman be capable of ovulating. Clomiphene is safer than treatment with human gonadotropins since there are fewer side effects and less risk of overstimulation. The main risk of clomiphene is the eventual presence of ovarian cysts which require that the treatment be discontinued. Clomiphene is given at first in doses of 50mg for five days starting on the fifth day of the cycle.

Pituitary Gonadotropin, the "Fertility Shots"

Ovulation can be produced by giving serial injections of pituitary gonadotropins over the early half of the menstrual cycle. These drugs can only be used in those women who have ovaries capable of responding but are not producing gonadotropins on their own. Most patients require daily injections of varying dosage starting on the fifth day of the cycle for about ten days. Eventually, once the ovary prepares to ovulate, subsequent injection of human chorionic gonadotropin, which is similar to another pituitary hormone, will produce ovulation. Careful monitoring of the patient is required with serial blood studies to help prevent overstimulation of the ovaries. Ovulation, using these techniques, can be achieved in about 75 percent of patients who previously did not ovulate. Perhaps, however, only half of these will eventually produce a pregnancy. But there is no question that these drugs have enabled many women to conceive who previously had no chance.

Artificial Insemination

When the male partner produces inadequate semen for fertilization and the female is healthy, some doctors recommend the use of donor sperm for insemination. In a large number of cases, we have found this procedure to be physically and emotionally successful and a practical alternative to adoption. This office procedure involves the placing of suitable donor sperm into the vagina at the time of ovulation. The success rate approaches that of normal sexual relations for conception.

In Vitro Fertilization

There are now some 200 babies born who have been produced in a "test tube." For women with closed tubes the process of in vitro fertilization enables, in some cases, a successful pregnancy. Ovums obtained by laparoscopy and fertilized by sperm in a test tube are placed back into the uterus for growth. At this time many centers are opening to carry out this process. There seems to be little question about its success and safety. This process offers new hope to many infertile couples.

16
PREGNANCY AND
THE OLDER WOMAN

In the past few years, there has been a 15 percent rise in the birth rate among women who once were thought to be slightly beyond their childbearing years. The 30- to 44-year-olds. What accounts for this phenomenon? One reason is that the 37 million pool of post-war baby-boom women is now 25 to 35 years old. As a group, these women marry later, and delay having children until their education is completed and their careers are established. Many are now having long postponed pregnancies. Many successful businesswomen, professionals, and even mothers of grown children have reconsidered pregnancy before the biological clock runs out. More and more career women are now deciding to have a family.

What are the important medical facts that will aid an older couple deciding on a family either now or in the future?

Pre-Partum Care

During the years prior to your first pregnancy, good gynecologic care is important. A yearly gynecologic exam and Pap smear will detect possible disorders which might eventually impair your ability to conceive. They include cervical dysplasia, uterine fibroids, pelvic endometriosis, and pelvic inflammation. Early treatment of these disorders should preserve subsequent fertility. Your physician may advise you not to wait too long if this is a problem.

Your choice of contraceptive during these years will also be guided to some extent by your plans. For example, an IUD (intrauterine device) can be associated with pelvic infection. This contraceptive method would probably be low on your list. Preparing for pregnancy by maintaining good health, nutrition, normal weight, and good fitness and exercise tolerance is also important.

German measles vaccination should also be performed if necessary and genetic screening as well. If intercurrent medical conditions, such as high blood pressure, diabetes, or anemia, should occur, you might discuss altering your plans.

"Preventive maintenance" is the key to successfully preserving fertility.

Becoming Pregnant

Fertility rates decrease somewhat with age. In a recent study in France, the fertility rate using artificial techniques dropped from 75 percent in ages 18 to 30 to 62 percent in ages 30 to 35, and 55 percent after age 35. These figures were used to urge women to reconsider earlier childbearing. However, a drop of 20 percent after age 35 is not so bad when you consider that the natural fertility rate is over 90 percent. Even if accurate this would lead to a 70 percent fertility rate over 35 years. Not bad!

I do urge couples, when the female is over 30 and the male over 45, to seek medical evaluation after only six months of attempting to conceive. Fertility evaluation and therapy does not differ in this group, but there is less time remaining for therapy.

Pregnancy Care

The risks of all clinically significant chromosomal abnormalities rises from about 2 per 1000 at the youngest maternal ages to about 2.6 per 1000 at age 30, 5.6 per 1000 at age 35, 15.8 per 1000 at age 40, and 53.7 per 1000 at age 45.

However, the use of genetic amniocentesis has dramatically altered the medical and emotional risks of bearing children after age 35. At least a couple can *know* and do something about it if there is a genetic abnormality. The development of amniocentesis has occurred concurrently with the sociological event of later childbirth and has helped couples make this choice.

The abortion of miscarriage rate also rises somewhat after age 35 but not dramatically (10 to 15 percent higher). Other studies have shown that the prenatal course, labor, and delivery are generally uncomplicated even in women 45 years of age or older in the absence of other medical problems such as high blood pressure and diabetes.

The advances in perinatal care outlined elsewhere in this book have enabled women of any age to have healthier babies.

The traditional view that pregnant women in their thirties were risky patients with many complications and requiring delivery by Cesarean section has changed. This reversal has come about because of advances in obstetrics and the higher quality of health in women of this age group in general. It's certainly never too late to try!

17
EPILOGUE

Now that you have read this book, you may be struck by the scope of knowledge in the field of obstetrics. Obstetrics has advanced a great deal in the past 20 years. Our knowledge has progressed to the point that the reproductive needs of a woman can be safely and successfully provided.

If a woman wants to conceive, knowledge of conception, fertility, and implantation is available.

If pregnancy is to be avoided, contraception and abortion techniques have been developed and are readily available.

Once pregnancy is established, the science of neonatology can be a great help in guaranteeing a healthy, normal baby.

Obstetrical prenatal care has advanced to the point where maternal mortality is practically zero.

Perinatal and pediatric care are lowering the infant perinatal mortality rates.

Advances in obstetrical analgesia, anesthesia, and in the Lamaze technique have made delivery a safe, often comfortable, and pleasant experience.

It's a great era to be an obstetrician and gynecologist.

It's a great era to be having a baby!

INDEX

ABOUT THE AUTHOR

SHELDON H. CHERRY is a practicing obstetrician and gynecologist at New York's Mount Sinai Hospital and is Associate Clinical Professor of Obstetrics and Gynecology at the Mount Sinai School of Medicine. He is a member of the American College of Obstetrics and Gynecology, the American College of Surgeons, and the New York Obstetrical Society.

A pioneering researcher in perinatology, he is the author of numerous scientific papers in obstetrics and gynecology and co-editor of the textbook *Medical, Surgical and Gynecologic Complications of Pregnancy*. Besides the first edition of *Understanding Pregnancy and Childbirth*, he has also written *The Menopause Myth* and *For Women of All Ages*. His work has been given feature coverage in many national magazines and television programs.

He is the father of four daughters and is an avid yachtsman and photographer.